A206

The Enlightenment

Illustration Book

Edited by Colin Cunningham and Gill Perry

First published in 1992 by
The Open University
Walton Hall
Milton Keynes
United Kingdom
MK7 6AA

ISBN 0 7492 1114 8

Edited, designed and typeset by The Open University.

This book forms part of an Open University course A206 *The Enlightenment.*

Printed and bound in the United Kingdom by Spin Offset

Index

Names List

Subject/Title List

Colour Plates

▲ ***Colour Plate 1*** *Sir Joshua Reynolds,* Theory, *1779, oil on canvas, 172.7 cm. x 172.7 cm. (Royal Academy of Arts)*

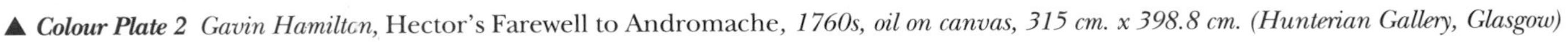

▲ ***Colour Plate 2*** *Gavin Hamilton,* Hector's Farewell to Andromache, *1760s, oil on canvas, 315 cm. x 398.8 cm. (Hunterian Gallery, Glasgow)*

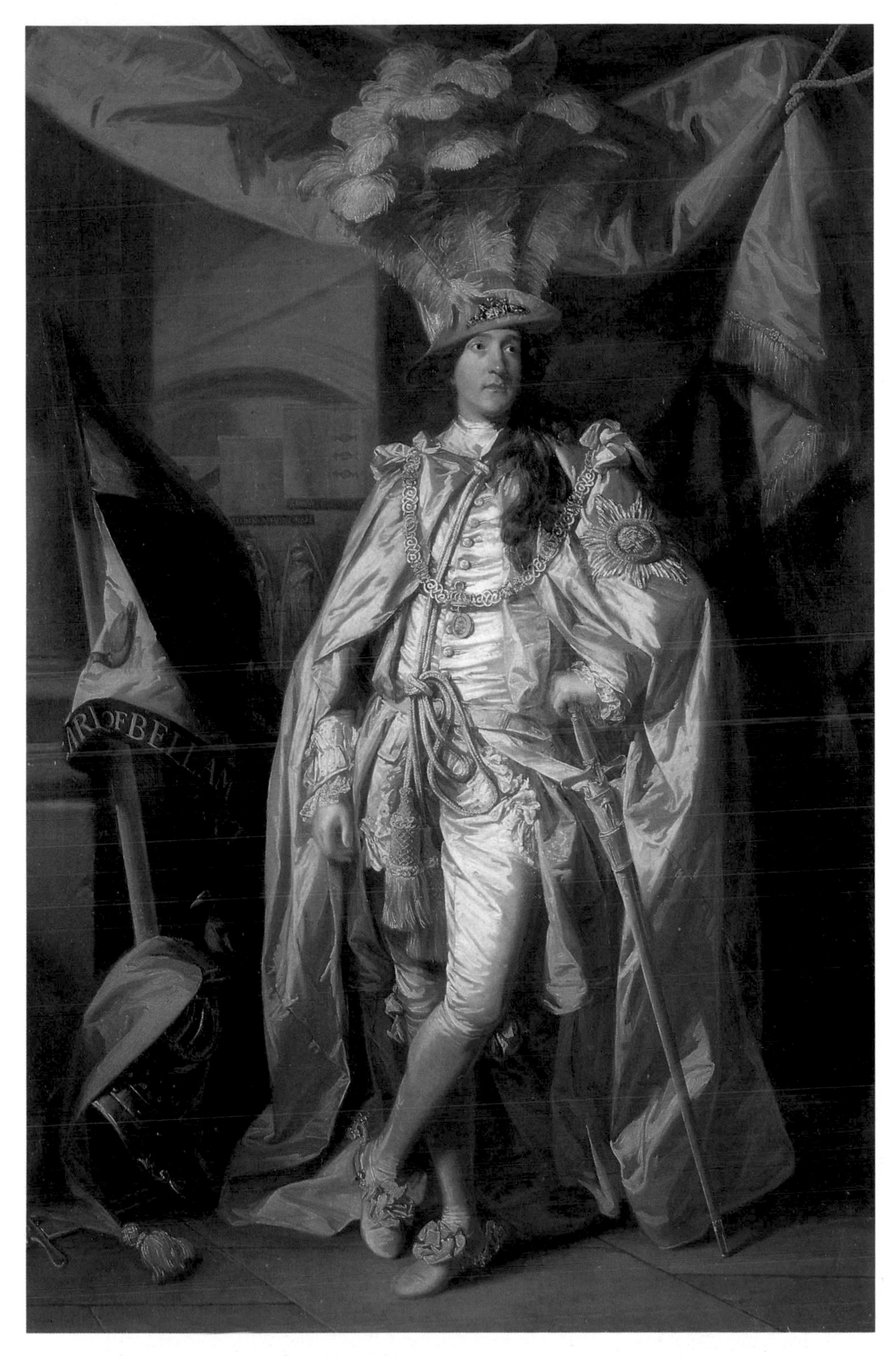

▲ ***Colour Plate 3*** *Sir Joshua Reynolds,* Charles Coote, 1st Earl of Bellamont *(1738–1800), oil on canvas, 245 cm. x 162 cm. (National Gallery of Ireland)*

▲ ***Colour Plate 4*** *Sir Joshua Reynolds,* Lady Sarah Bunbury sacrificing to the Graces, *1765, oil on canvas, 242 cm. x 151.5 cm. (Art Institute of Chicago, Mr and Mrs W.W. Kimball Collection, 1922. Photograph* c.*1990, The Art Institute of Chicago. All Rights Reserved.)*

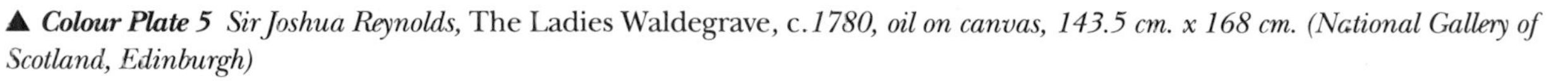

▲ ***Colour Plate 5*** *Sir Joshua Reynolds,* The Ladies Waldegrave, c.*1780, oil on canvas, 143.5 cm. x 168 cm. (National Gallery of Scotland, Edinburgh)*

▲ ***Colour Plate 6*** *Sir Joshua Reynolds,* The Montgomery Sisters adorning a Term of Hymen, *1773, oil on canvas, 233.7 cm. x 290.8 cm. (Tate Gallery, London)*

▲ ***Colour Plate 7*** *Sir Joshua Reynolds,* Mrs Hale as Euphrosyne, *1764–6, oil on canvas, 236cm. x 146 cm. (Reproduced by permission of the Earl of Harewood. Photo: Royal Academy of Arts)*

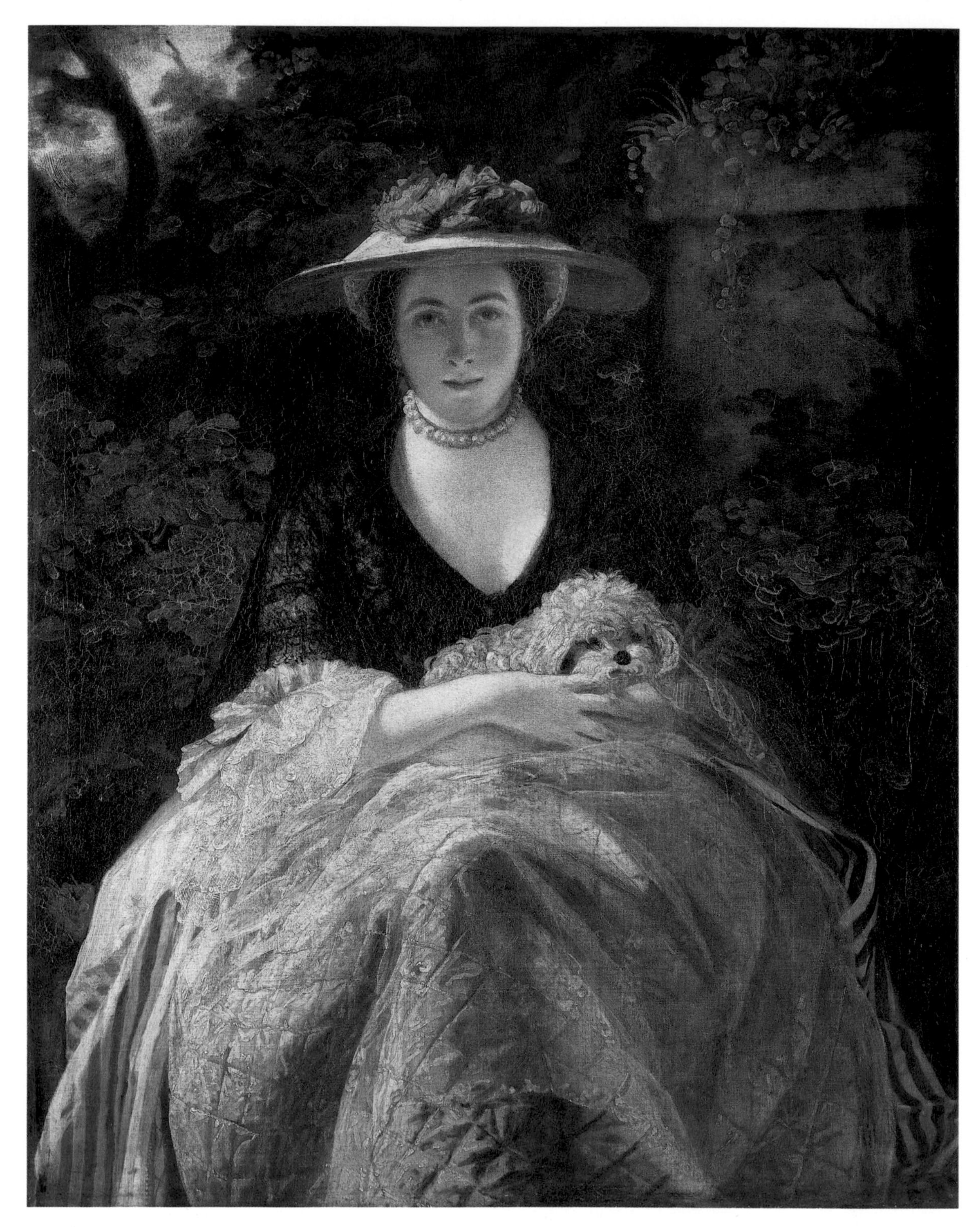

▲ ***Colour Plate 8*** *Sir Joshua Reynolds,* Nelly O'Brien, *1760–2. (Trustees of the Wallace Collection)*

▲ ***Colour Plate 9*** *Johann Zoffany,* The Academicians of the Royal Academy, *1771–2. (Reproduced by gracious permission of Her Majesty the Queen)*

▲ ***Colour Plate 10*** *Syon House, Ante Room. (A. F. Kersting)*

◀ **Colour Plate 11** *Syon House, Gallery, detail. (A. F. Kersting)*

▲ **Colour Plate 12** *Robert Adam, alternative designs for the Gallery at Syon House. (The Trustees of Sir John Soane's Museum)*

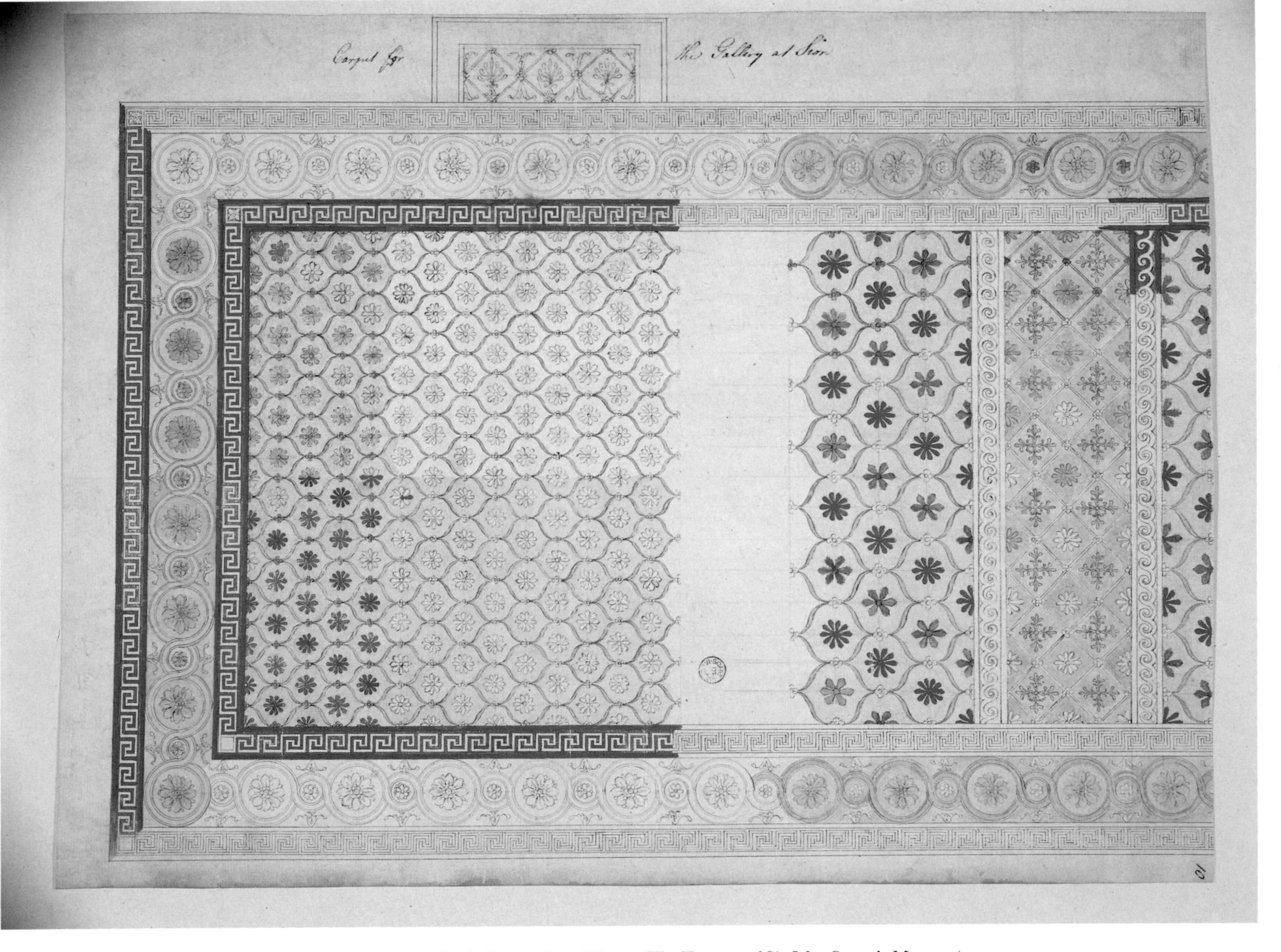

▲ **Colour Plate 13** *Robert Adam, design for the carpet in the Gallery at Syon House. (The Trustees of Sir John Soane's Museum)*

▲ **Colour Plate 14** *Kedleston Hall, State Drawing Room. (National Trust Photographic Library)*

▲ **Colour Plate 15** *Robert Adam, design for the Dining Room Ceiling at Kedleston, 1762. (National Trust Photographic Library)*

▲ **Colour Plate 16** *Robert Adam, section of the Library at Kedleston for Lord Scarsdale. (The Trustees of Sir John Soane's Museum)*

▲ **Colour Plate 17** *Robert Adam, Ceiling for a new intended Bookroom at Kedleston. (The Trustees of Sir John Soane's Museum)*

▲ **Colour Plate 18** *Robert Adam, design for the proposed Bookroom at Kedleston. (The Trustees of Sir John Soane's Museum)*

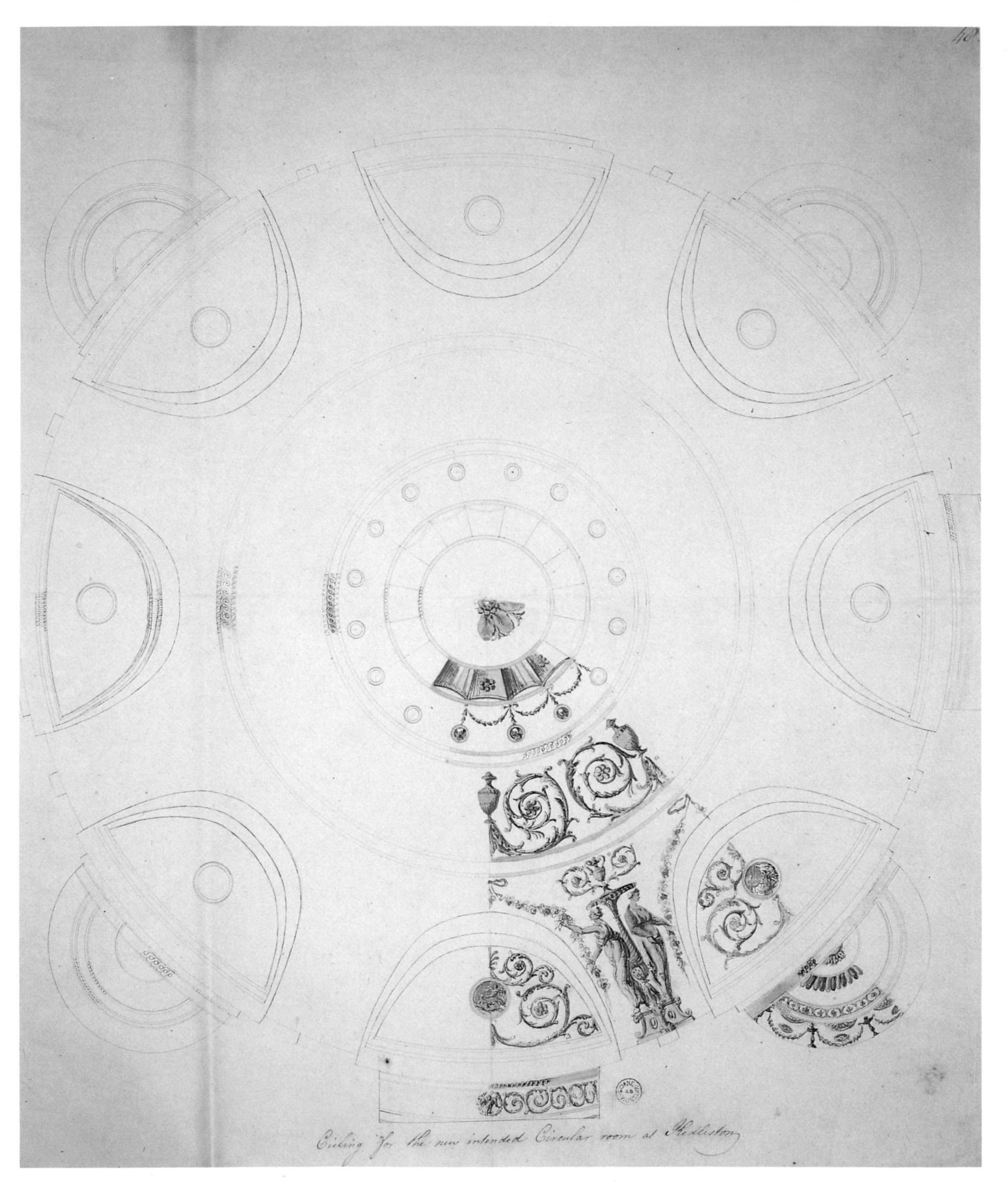

▲ ***Colour Plate 19*** *Robert Adam, Ceiling for the new intended Circular Room at Kedleston, 1768. (The Trustees of Sir John Soane's Museum)*

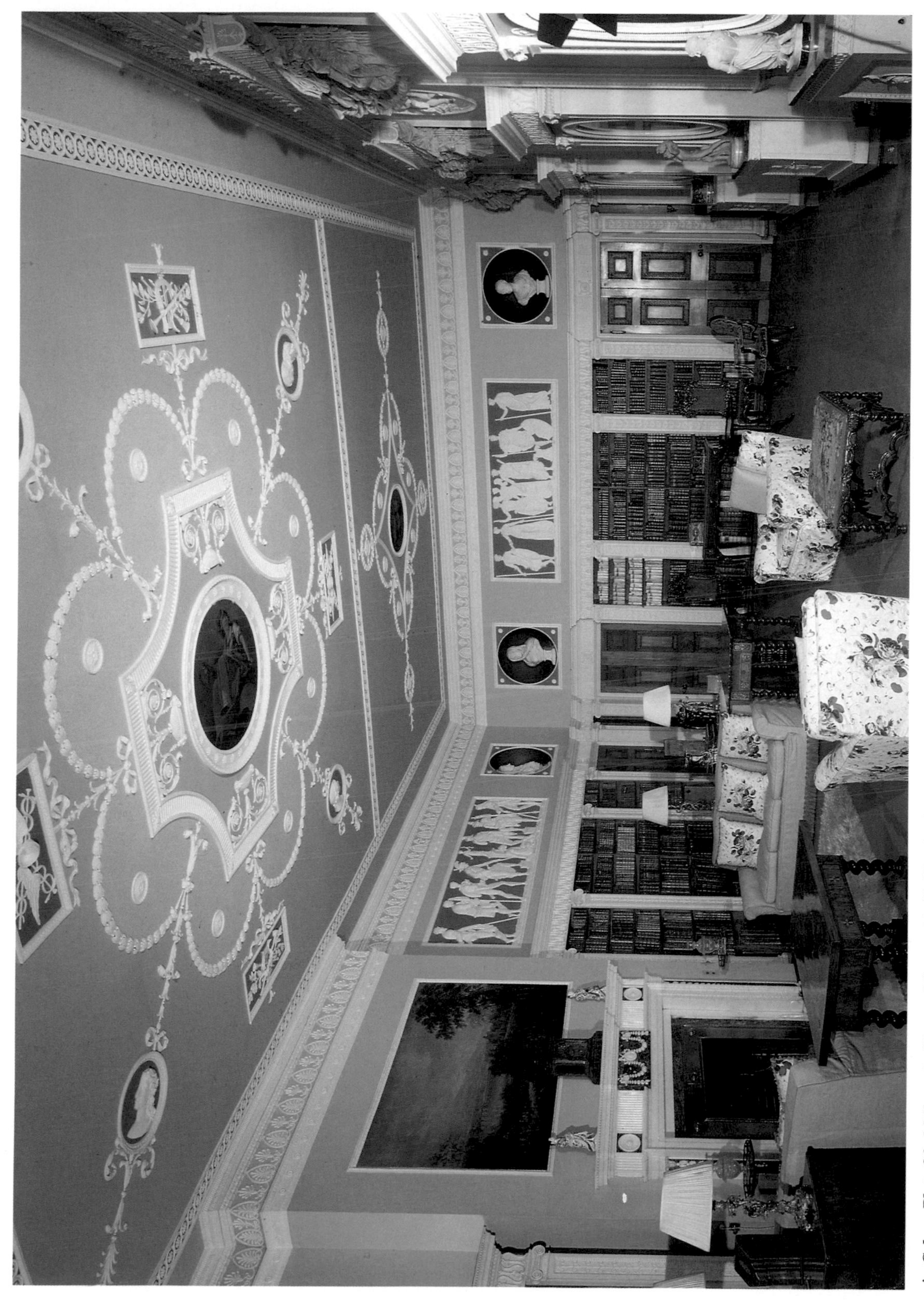

▲ **Colour Plate 20** *Mellerstain House, Library. (A. F. Kersting)*

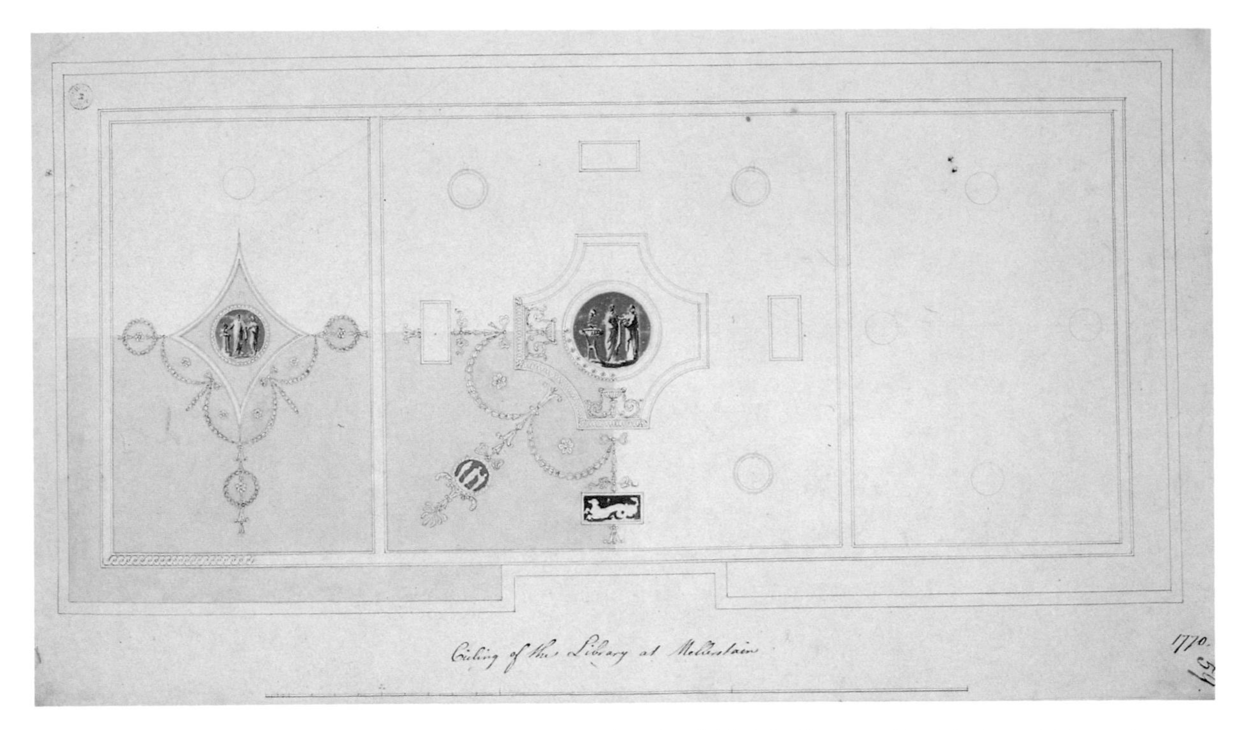

▲ ***Colour Plate 21*** *Robert Adam, Ceiling of the Library at Mellerstain, 1770. (The Trustees of Sir John Soane's Museum)*

▲ ***Colour Plate 22*** *Robert Adam, design for a sofa for Lord Scarsdale and also executed for Mrs Montagu in Hill Street, 1762. (The Trustees of Sir John Soane's Museum)*

▲ ***Colour Plate 23*** *J-S Chardin,* The Attributes of Music, *1765, oil on canvas, 91 cm. x 145 cm. (Louvre. Photo: Réunion des Musées Nationaux)*

▲ ***Colour Plate 24*** *F. Boucher,* Jove in the shape of Diana, surprises Callisto, *1769, oil on canvas, 160 cm. x 130 cm. (Wallace Collection, London)*

▲ ***Colour Plate 25*** *J-S Chardin,* The Scullery Maid, *1738, oil on canvas, 45.4 cm. x 37 cm. (Hunterian Art Gallery, Glasgow)*

▲ ***Colour Plate 26*** *J-S Chardin,* Third Picture of Refreshments, *1764, oil on canvas, 152.5 cm. x 96.5 cm. (James Philip Gray Collection, Museum of Fine Arts, Springfield, MA.)*

▲ ***Colour Plate 27*** *J-S Chardin,* A Basket of Grapes, *1764, oil on canvas, 32 cm. x 40 cm. (Musée d'Angers)*

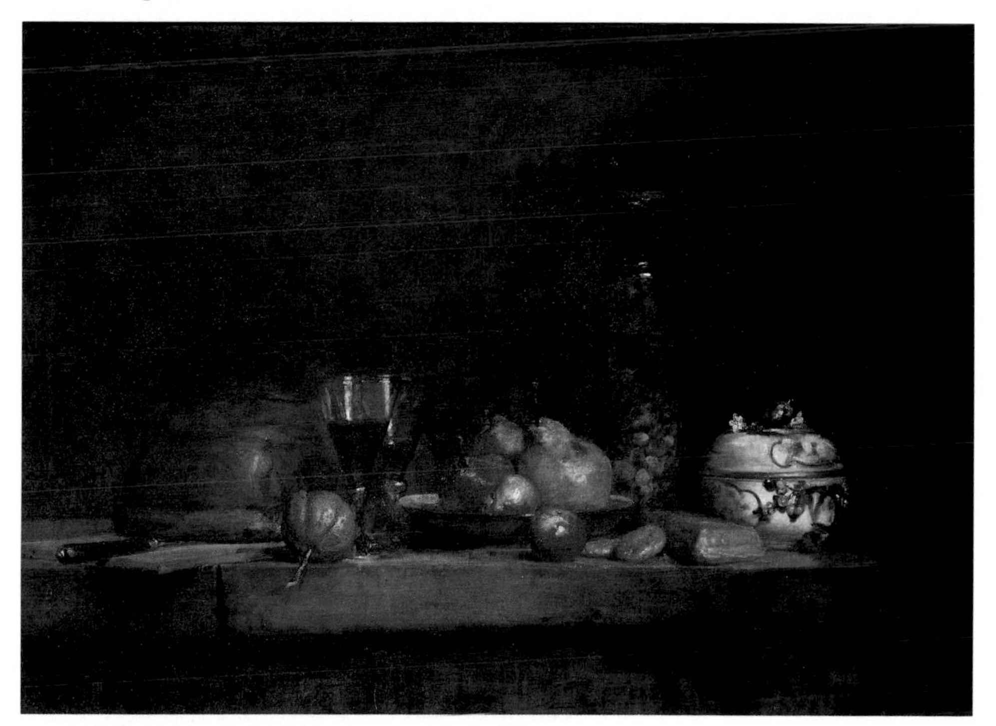

▲ ***Colour Plate 28*** *J-S Chardin,* The Jar of Olives, *1760, oil on canvas, 71 cm. x 98 cm. (Louvre. Photo: Réunion des Musées Nationaux)*

▶ ***Colour Plate 29***
J-S Chardin, The Rayfish,
c.*1726, oil on canvas,*
114 cm. x 146 cm.
(Louvre. Photo: Réunion des Musées Nationaux)

(detail)

(detail)

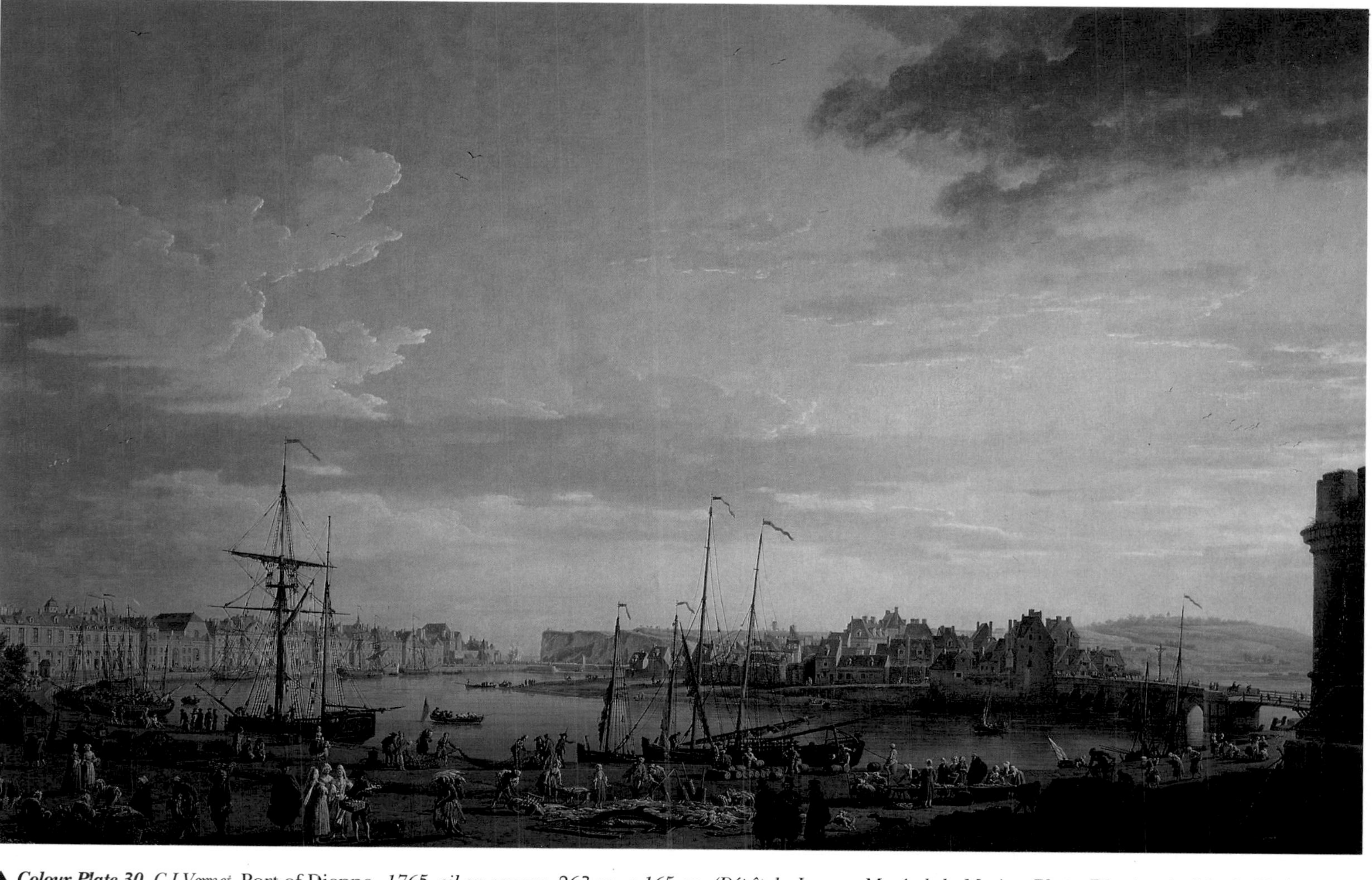

▲ ***Colour Plate 30*** *C-J Vernet*, Port of Dieppe, *1765, oil on canvas, 263 cm. x 165 cm. (Dépôt du Louvre, Musée de la Marine. Photo: Réunion des Musées Nationaux)*

▲ ***Colour Plate 31*** *J-B Greuze,* The Young Girl Crying over Her Dead Bird, *oil on canvas, 53.6 cm. x 46.3 cm. (National Gallery of Scotland)*

Black and White Plates

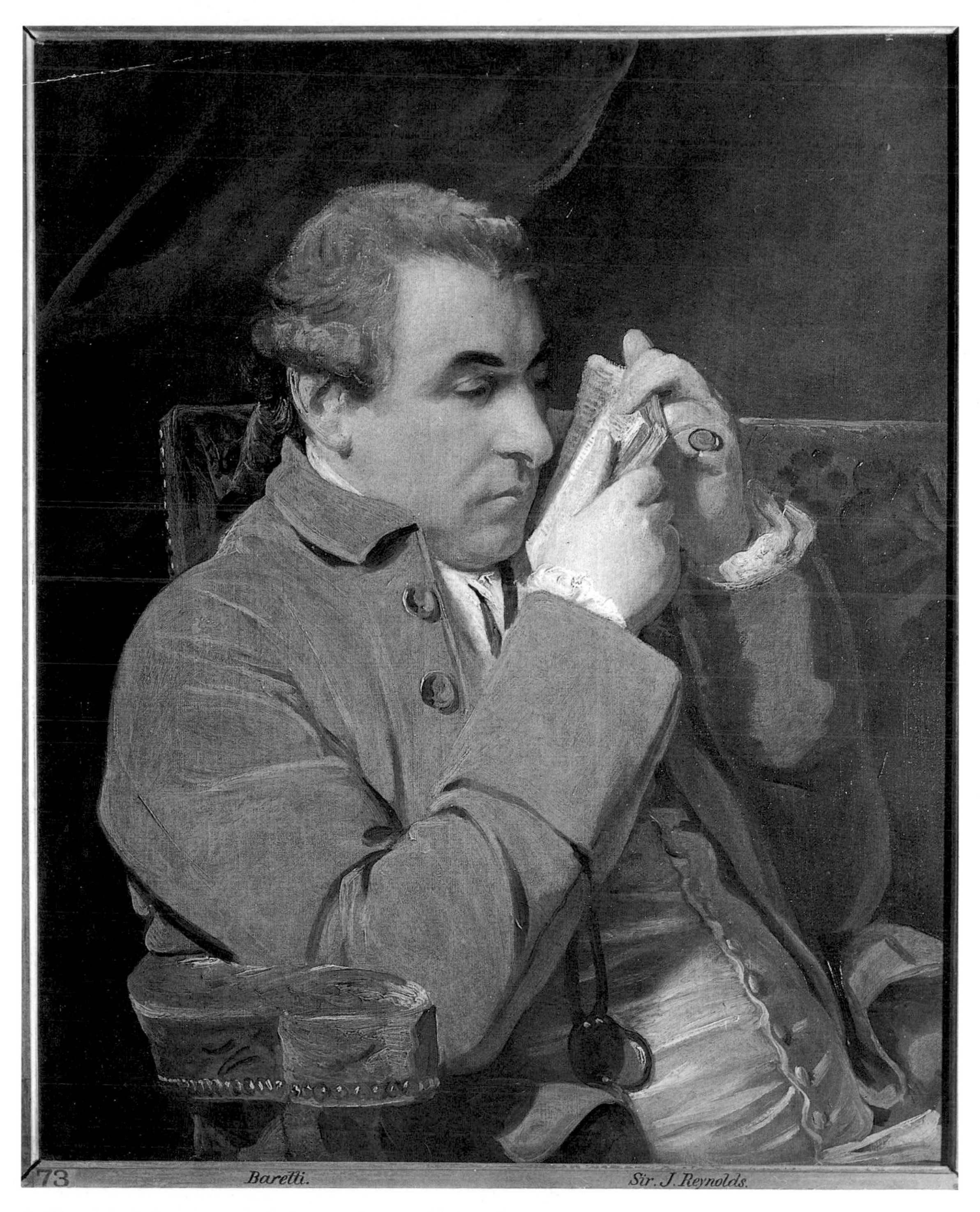

▲ **Plate 1** *Sir Joshua Reynolds,* Guiseppe Baretti, *1773, oil on canvas, 73.7 cm. x 62.2 cm. (Private Collection)*

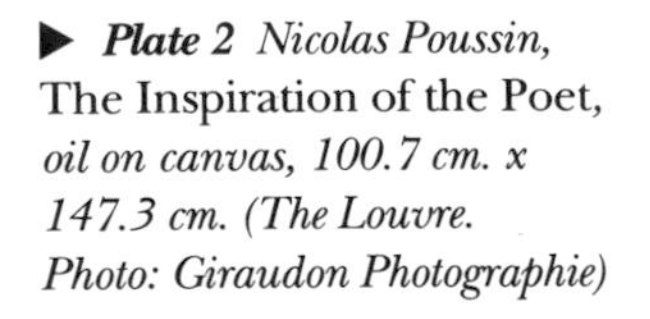

▶ ***Plate 2*** *Nicolas Poussin,* The Inspiration of the Poet, *oil on canvas, 100.7 cm. x 147.3 cm. (The Louvre. Photo: Giraudon Photographie)*

▶ ***Plate 3*** *Sir Joshua Reynolds,* Dr James Beattie: 'The Triumph of Truth', *oil on canvas, 122 cm. x 155 cm. (University of Aberdeen)*

▲ ***Plate 4*** *Sir Joshua Reynolds,* Fortitude, *1777–8, oil on canvas, 223.5 cm. x 83.8 cm. (Private Collection, Photo: Royal Academy of Arts)*

▲ ***Plate 5*** *Sir Joshua Reynolds,* Justice, *1777–8, oil on canvas, 223.5 cm. x 83.8 cm. (Private Collection. Photo: Royal Academy of Arts)*

▲ ***Plate 6*** *Sir Joshua Reynolds,* Commodore Augustus Keppel, *1752–3 oil on canvas, 238.8 cm. x 147 cm. (National Maritime Museum, London)*

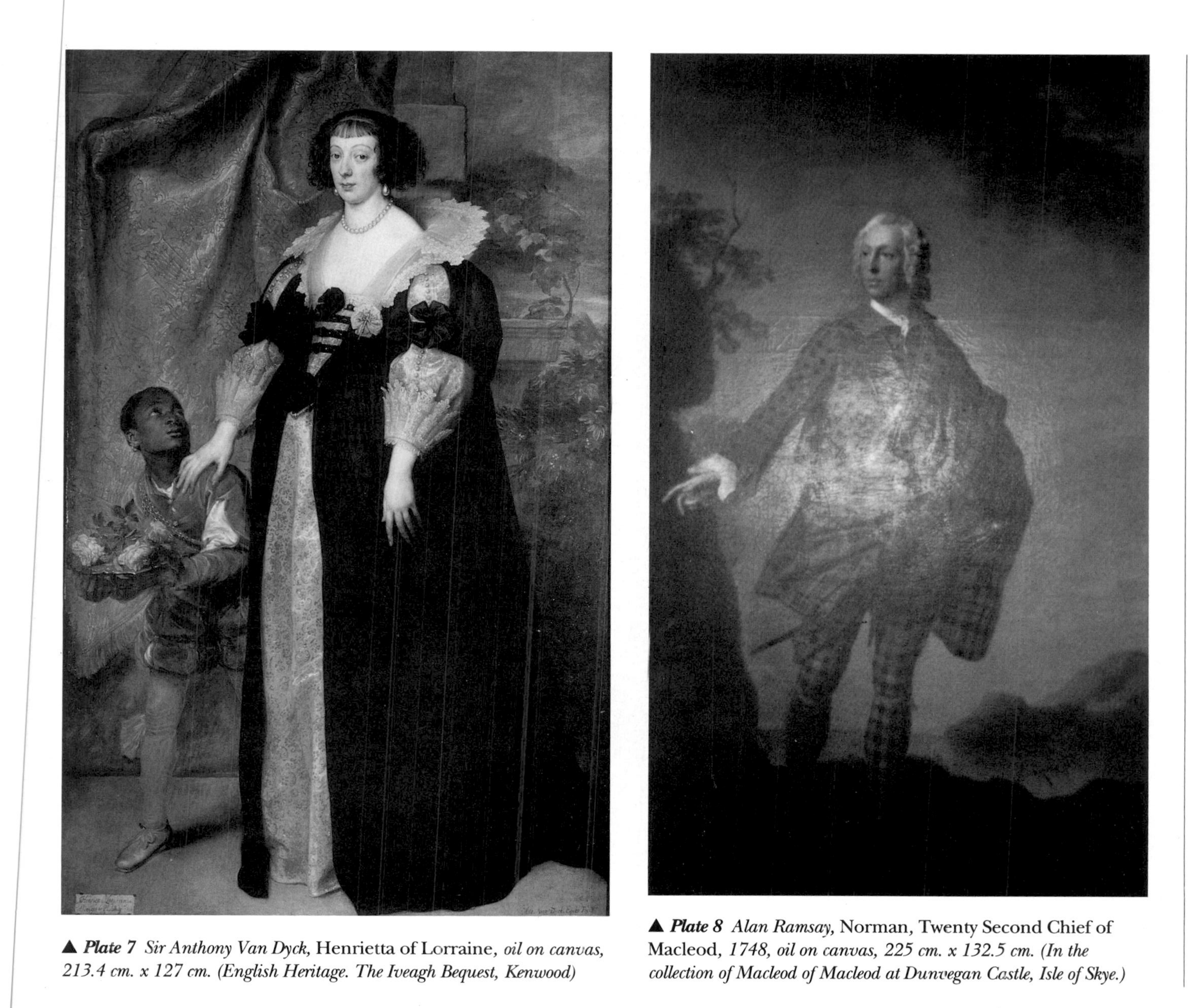

▲ ***Plate 7*** *Sir Anthony Van Dyck,* Henrietta of Lorraine, *oil on canvas, 213.4 cm. x 127 cm. (English Heritage. The Iveagh Bequest, Kenwood)*

▲ ***Plate 8*** *Alan Ramsay,* Norman, Twenty Second Chief of Macleod, *1748, oil on canvas, 225 cm. x 132.5 cm. (In the collection of Macleod of Macleod at Dunvegan Castle, Isle of Skye.)*

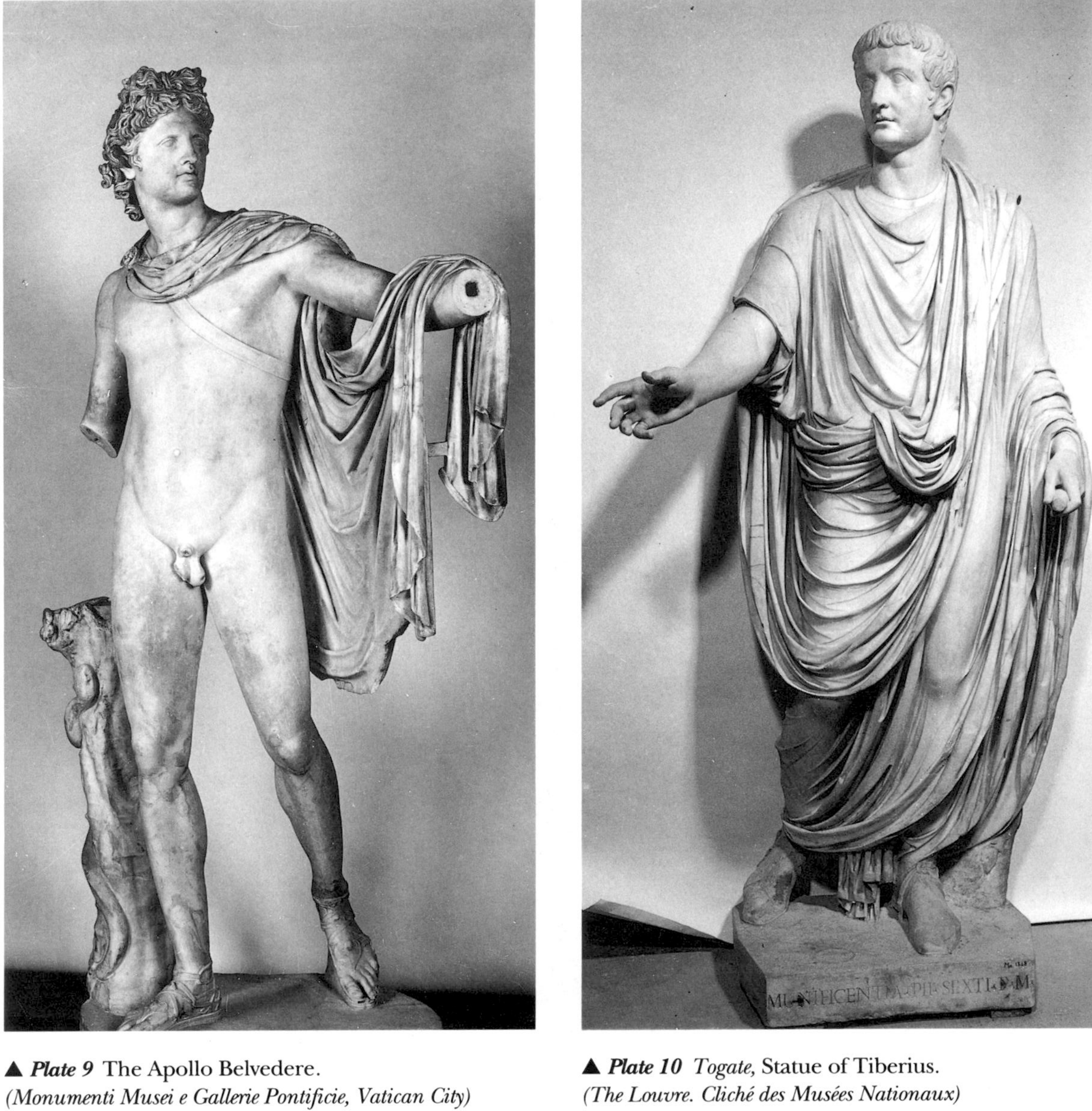

▲ ***Plate 9*** The Apollo Belvedere.
(Monumenti Musei e Gallerie Pontificie, Vatican City)

▲ ***Plate 10*** *Togate*, Statue of Tiberius.
(The Louvre. Cliché des Musées Nationaux)

▲ ***Plate 11*** *Sir Joshua Reynolds,* Mrs Siddons as the Tragic Muse, *1789, oil on canvas, 239.7 cm. x 147.6 cm. (Dulwich Picture Gallery, London)*

▲ ***Plate 12*** *Sir Joshua Reynolds,* The Countess Spencer with her Daughter, *oil on canvas. (The Earl Spencer, Althorp. Photo: Royal Academy of Arts)*

▲ ***Plate 13*** *Sir Joshua Reynolds,* Anne, Countess of Albermarle, *oil on canvas, 125.5 cm. x 101 cm. (National Gallery, London)*

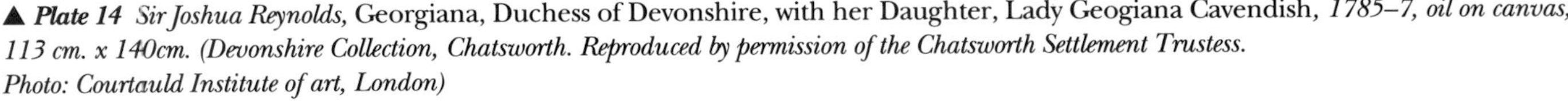

▲ **Plate 14** *Sir Joshua Reynolds,* Georgiana, Duchess of Devonshire, with her Daughter, Lady Geogiana Cavendish, *1785–7, oil on canvas, 113 cm. x 140cm. (Devonshire Collection, Chatsworth. Reproduced by permission of the Chatsworth Settlement Trustess. Photo: Courtauld Institute of art, London)*

▲ ***Plate 15*** *Sir Joshua Reynolds,* Mrs Richard Hoare with her Son, *oil on canvas, 132.5 cm. x 101.6cm. (Trustees of the Wallace Collection, London)*

▲ ***Plate 16*** *Sir Joshua Reynolds,* Philip Gell, *oil on canvas, 236 cm. x 145cm. (Lt.Col John Chandos-Pole. Photo: Paul Mellon Centre for Studies in British Art)*

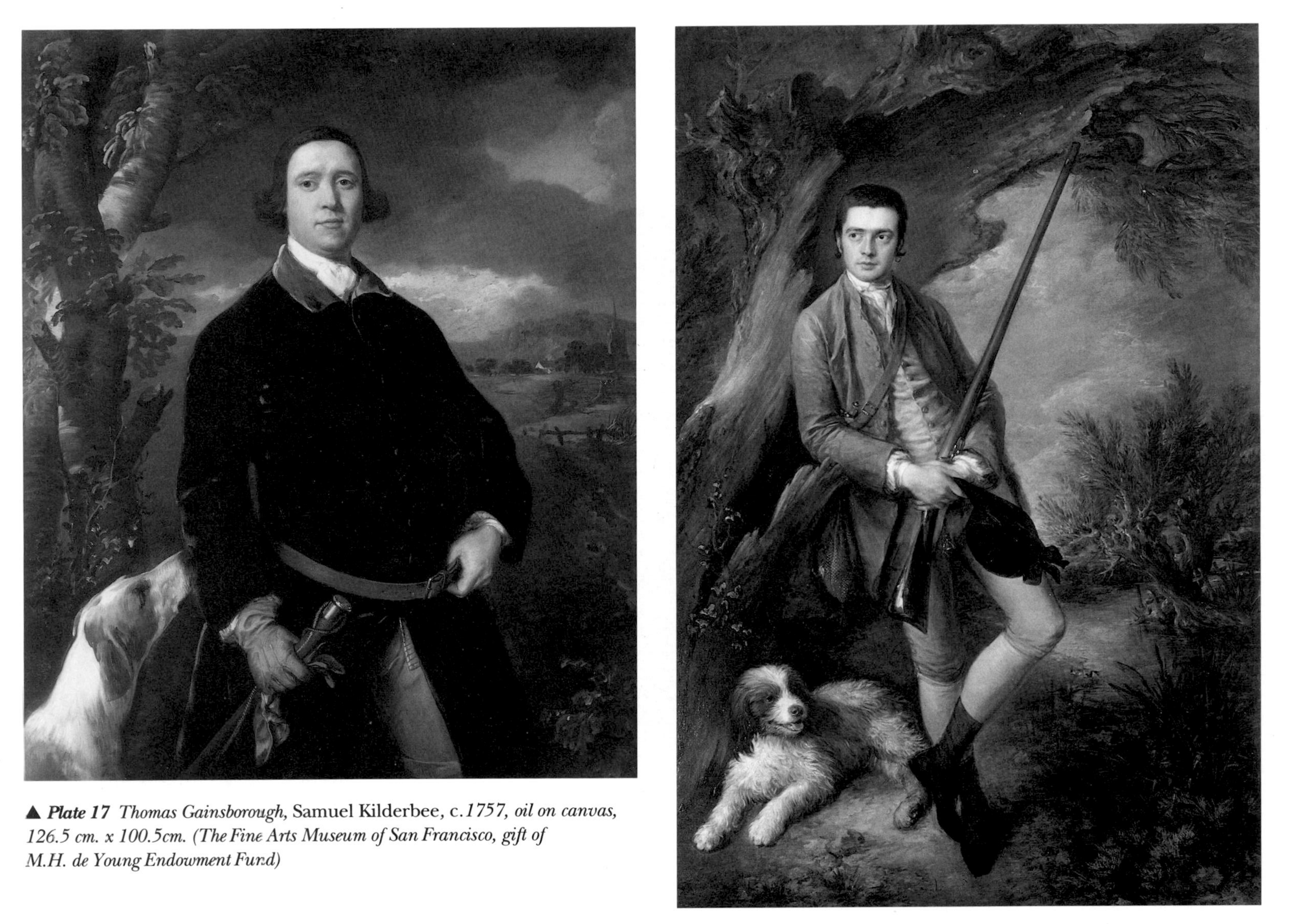

▲ **Plate 17** *Thomas Gainsborough,* Samuel Kilderbee, *c.1757, oil on canvas, 126.5 cm. x 100.5cm. (The Fine Arts Museum of San Francisco, gift of M.H. de Young Endowment Fund)*

▲ **Plate 18** *Thomas Gainsborough,* William Poyntz, *1762, oil on canvas, 231.5 cm. x 150cm. (The Earl Spencer, Althorp)*

▲ ***Plate 19*** *Thomas Gainsborough,* Mrs Mary Robinson ('Perdita'), *oil on canvas, 233.7 cm. x 153cm. (Trustees of the Wallace Collection, London)*

▲ ***Plate 20*** *Sir Joshua Reynolds,* Miss Kitty Fisher, *1759, oil on canvas, 75 cm. x 62.8cm. (The National Trust, Petworth, Egremont Collection)*

▲ **Plate 21** *Angelica Kauffman,* Venus persuading Helen to love Paris, *1790. (Hermitage Museum, St Petersburg)*

▲ ***Plate 22*** *Sir Joshua Reynolds*, Members of the Society of Dilettanti, *1778, oil on canvas, 196.8 cm. x 142.2cm. (The Society of Dilettanti. Photo: Royal Academy of Arts)*

▲ ***Plate 23*** *Sir Joshua Reynolds*, Members of the Society of Dilettanti, *1778, oil on canvas, 196.8 cm. x 142.2cm. (The Society of Dilettanti. Photo: Royal Academy of Arts)*

The captions of the Engravings (in separate folder) and Plates 36–47 use Adam's original words.

▲ ***Plate 24*** *Portrait of Robert Adam by George Wilson,* c.*1773.*

▶ **Plate 25** *Rome, Arch of Constantine, completed* AD *315. (Archivi Alinari, Florence)*

▶ **Plate 26** *Split, Palace of Diocletian,* c. AD *300–6. (Mansell Collection)*

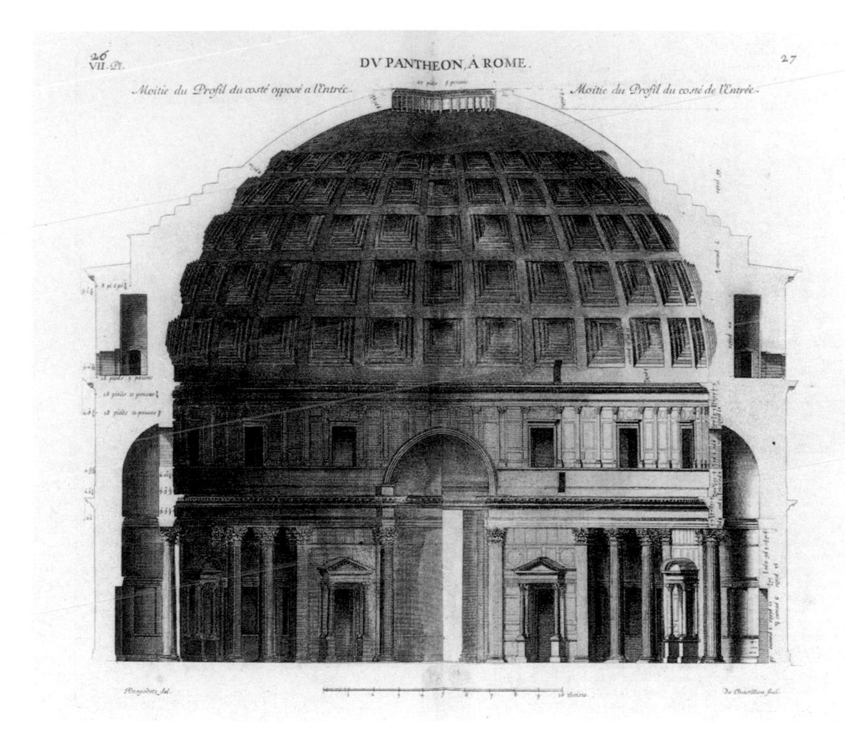

▲ ***Plate 27*** *Rome, Pantheon,* AD *118–*c.*128: section through dome from Desgodetz,* Les Edifices Antiques de Rome *(1682). (British Library)*

▲ ***Plate 28*** *Tivoli, Hadrian's villa, remains of dome,* AD *118–125. (Sopr. Arch. Lazio)*

▲ **Plate 29** *Rome, Temple of Fortuna Virilis,* c.*100* BC. *(Mansell Collection)*

▲ **Plate 30** *Athens, Erechtheion, north porch,* c.*421–405* BC. *(Mansell Collection)*

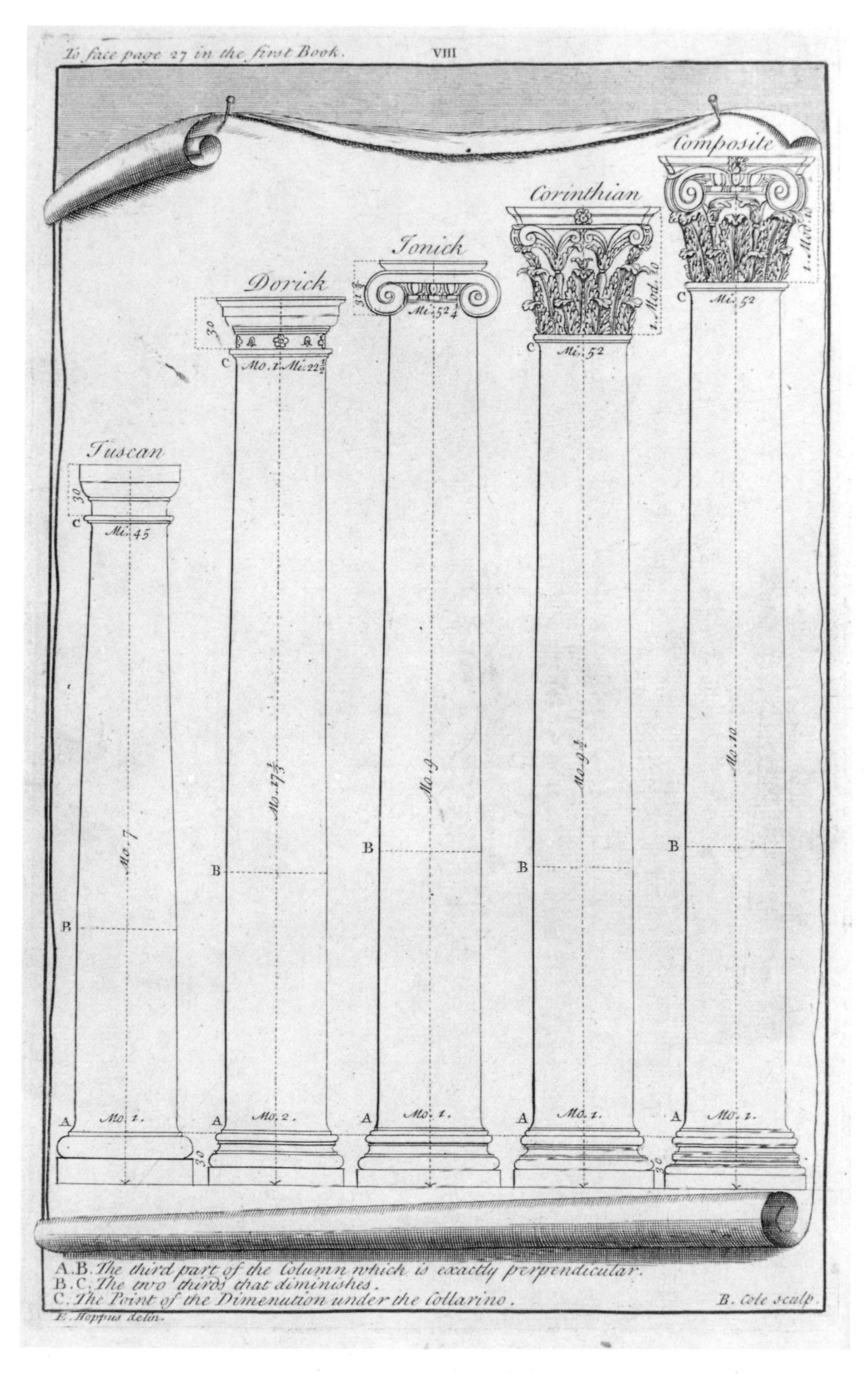

▲ ***Plate 31*** *Andrea Palladio,* I Quattro Libri dell' Architettura *('Four Books on Architecture'), ed. Hoppus, 1733. (Each column is shown with base, shaft and capital, but the entablatures are not drawn.) (Photo by permission of the Syndics of Cambridge University Library)*

▶ ***Plate 32*** *Rome, St Peter's: dome, designed by Michelangelo, 1558–60 and completed by Giacomo della Porta, 1588–90. The façade was by Carlo Maderna* c.*1607–15 and the colonnades by Bernini 1656ff. (Archivi Alinari, Florence)*

▼ ***Plate 33*** *London, Greenwich, the Queen's House, south front, Inigo Jones, 1616–35. (Royal Commission on the Historical Monuments of England)*

▲ *Plate 34 Blenheim Palace, Oxon., built for the Duke of Marlborough, 1705ff. Entrance façade, from an early eighteenth-century engraving. (Mansell Collection)*

▲ ***Plate 35*** *R. Adam,* Ruins of the Palace of the Emperor Diocletian at Spalatro, *1764, Frontispiece. (Copyright: RIBA)*

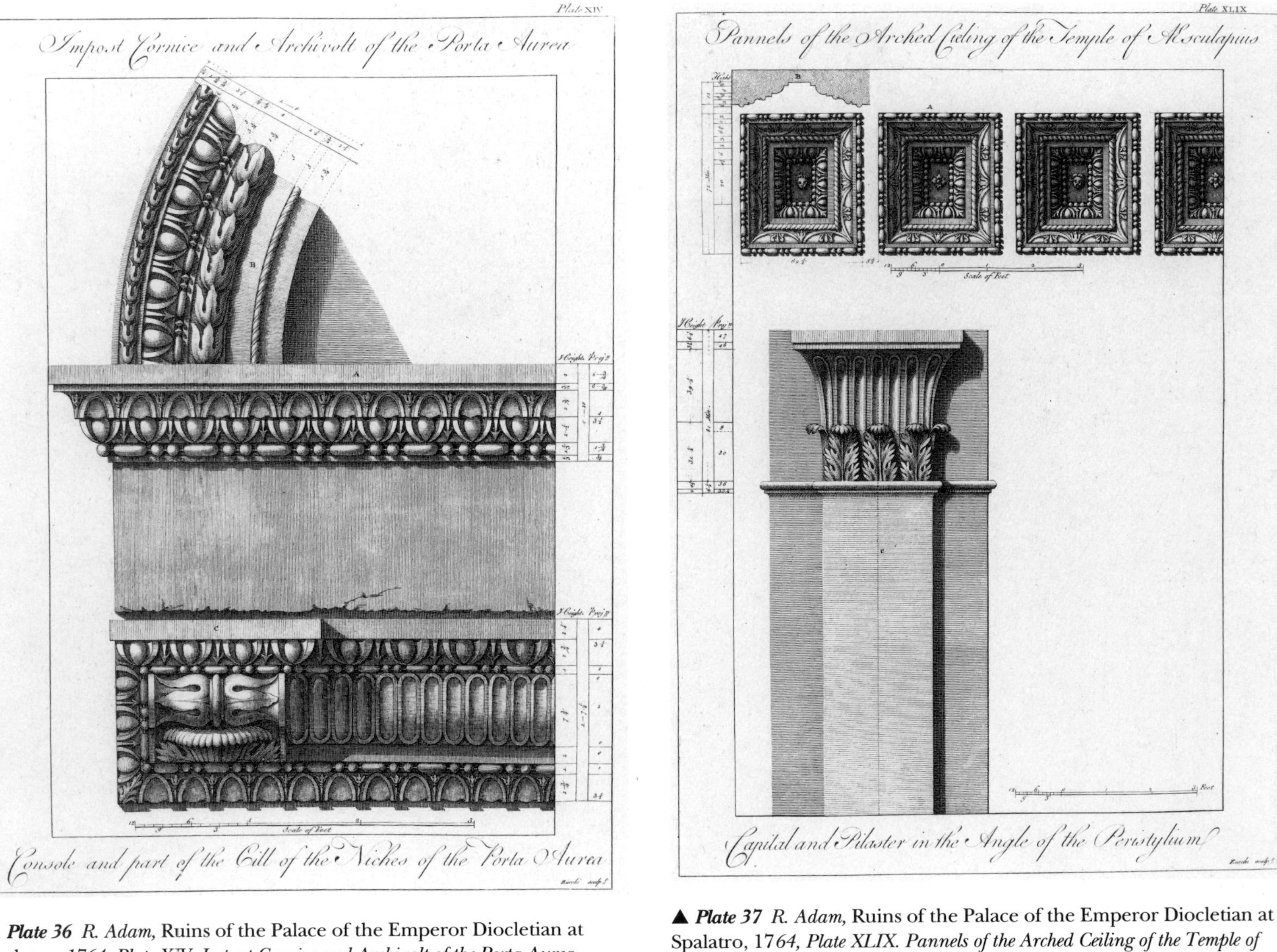

▲ ***Plate 36*** *R. Adam,* Ruins of the Palace of the Emperor Diocletian at Spalatro, *1764, Plate XIV. Impost Cornice and Archivolt of the Porta Aurea. (Copyright: RIBA)*

▲ ***Plate 37*** *R. Adam,* Ruins of the Palace of the Emperor Diocletian at Spalatro, 1764, *Plate XLIX. Pannels of the Arched Ceiling of the Temple of Aesculapius: Capital and Pilaster in the Angle of the Peristylium. (Copyright: RIBA)*

▲ ***Plate 38*** The Works in Architecture of Robert and James Adam, *Frontispiece, 1773. (Copyright: RIBA)*

▲ ***Plate 39*** *R. Adam,* Works *I. v. (ii), design of the entablature and Britannic Order for the Gateway proposed for Carleton House, 1767. (Copyright: RIBA)*

▲ ***Plate 40*** *R. Adam,* Works *II. iii. (vii), design of a Bridge in imitation of the Aqueducts of the Ancients proposed to be built over the Lake at Bowood Park in Wiltshire, 1768 (pub.1778). (Copyright: RIBA)*

◀ ***Plate 41*** *R. Adam,* Works *I. v. (v), original design of an Illumination and Transparency part of which was executed by command of the Queen in June 1762 In Honour of His Majesty's Birthday. (Copyright: RIBA)*

▶ ***Plate 42*** R. Adam, Works *III. xxi, inside view of the Supper room & part of the Ball-room in a Pavilion erected for a Fète Champêtre in the Garden of the Earl of Derby at the Oaks in Surry, the 9th, of June, 1774. (Copyright: RIBA)*

▶ ***Plate 43*** R. Adam, Works *III. xxii, inside view of the Ball-room erected for a Fète Champêtre in the Garden of the Earl of Derby at the Oaks Surry, the 9th of June, 1774. (Copyright: RIBA)*

▲ **Plate 44** R. Adam, Works *II. i. (vi), Chimney piece for the Countess of Derby's Etruscan Dressing room, of white marble inlaid with Ornaments of Scagliola in the Etruscan taste, with Glass frame over it, 1773 (pub.1777). (Copyright: RIBA)*

▲ **Plate 45** *R. Adam,* Works *I. v. (viii), design of a Harpsichord, inlaid with various-coloured woods, executed in London for the Empress of Russia, 1771 (pub.1773). (Copyright: RIBA)*

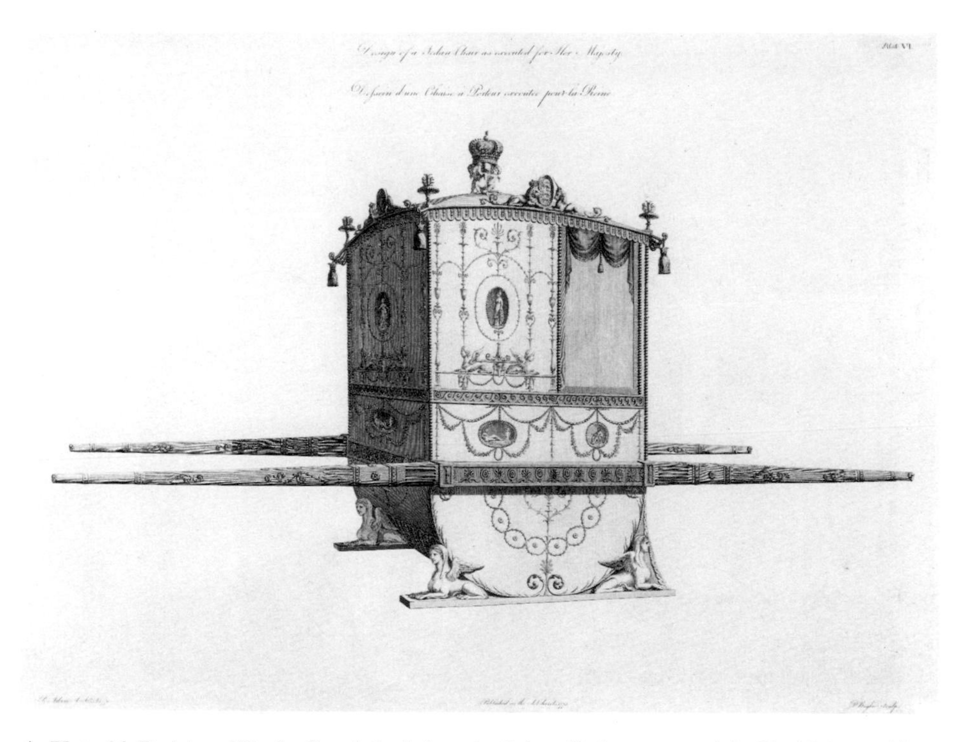

▲ ***Plate 46*** R. Adam, Works *I. v. (vi), design of a Sedan-Chair as executed for Her Majesty, 1771 (pub.1773). (Copyright: RIBA)*

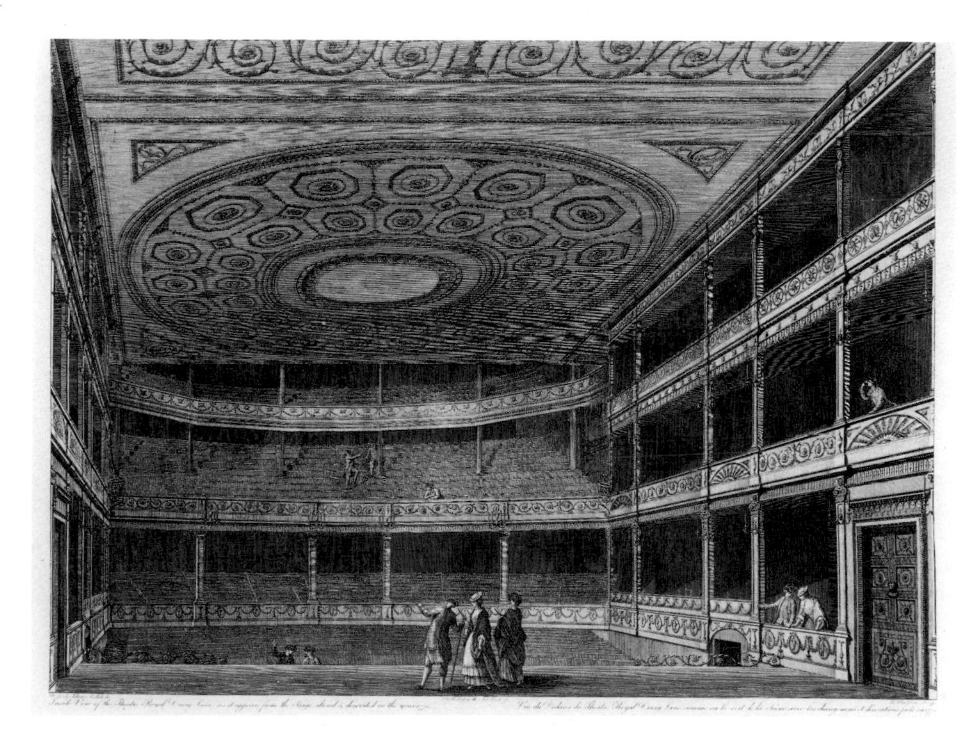

▲ ***Plate 47*** R. Adam, Works *II. v. (vii), inside view of the Theatre Royal, Drury Lane as it appears from the stage, altered and decorated in the year 1775 (pub.1779). (Copyright: RIBA)*

▲ **Plate 48** *Syon House, Brentford, 1762–9, entrance front with inner lodges. (Royal Commission on the Historical Monuments of England)*

▲ **Plate 49** *Syon House, Brentford, interior of courtyard. (Royal Commission on the Historical Monuments of England)*

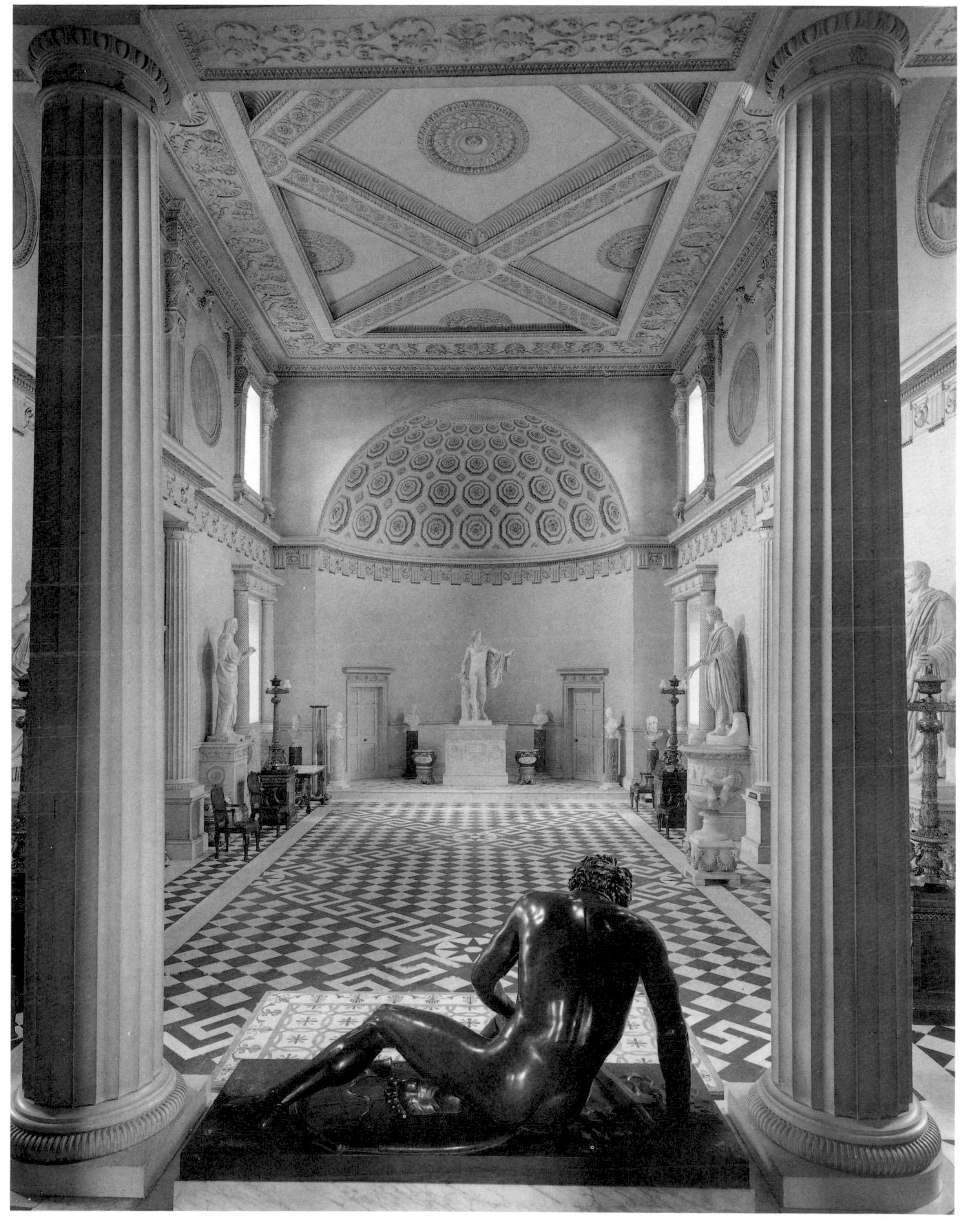

▲ ***Plate 50*** *Syon House, Brentford, Hall, general view. (A. F. Kersting)*

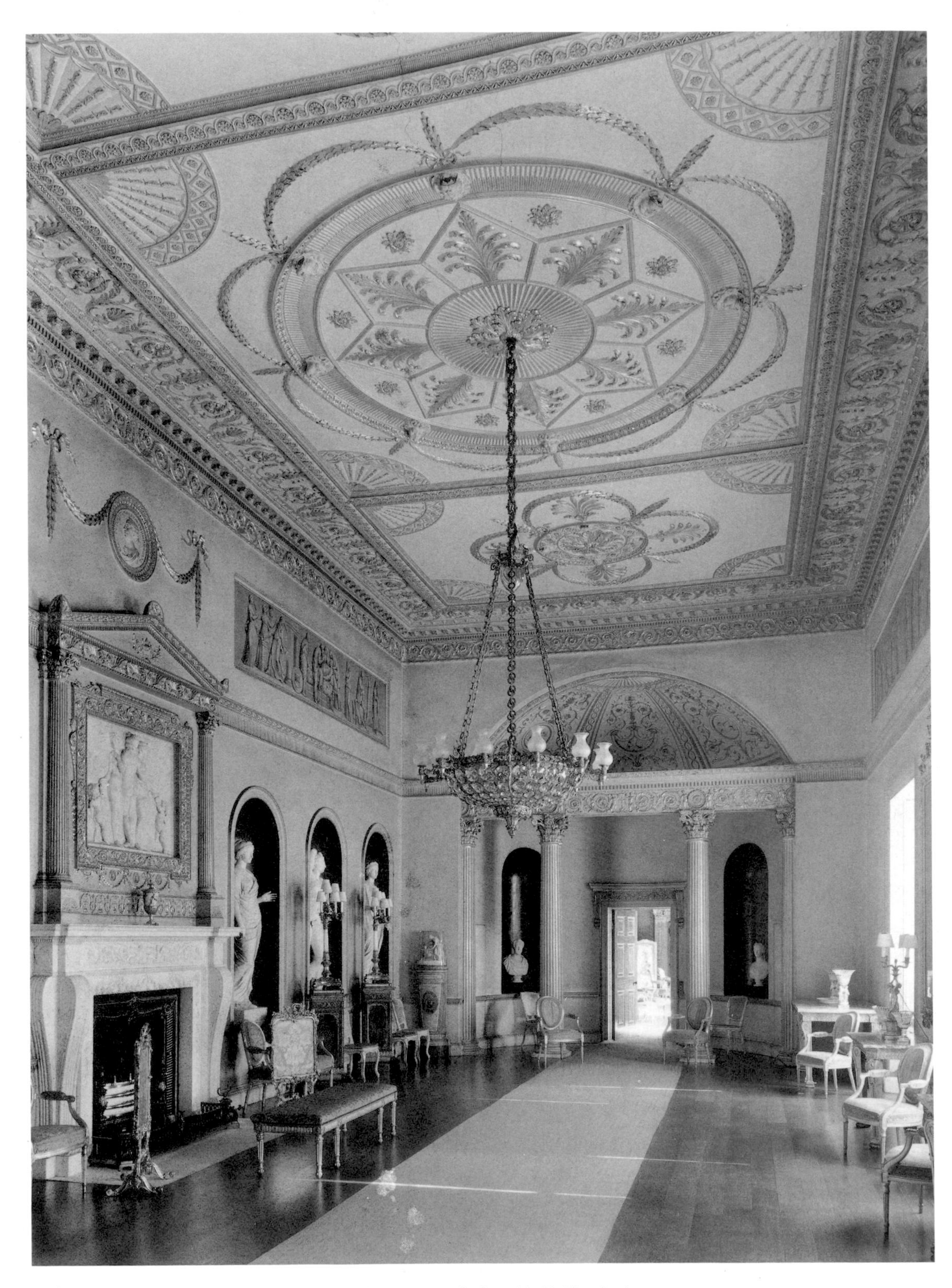

▲ ***Plate 51*** *Syon House, Brentford, Dining Room, general view. (A. F. Kersting)*

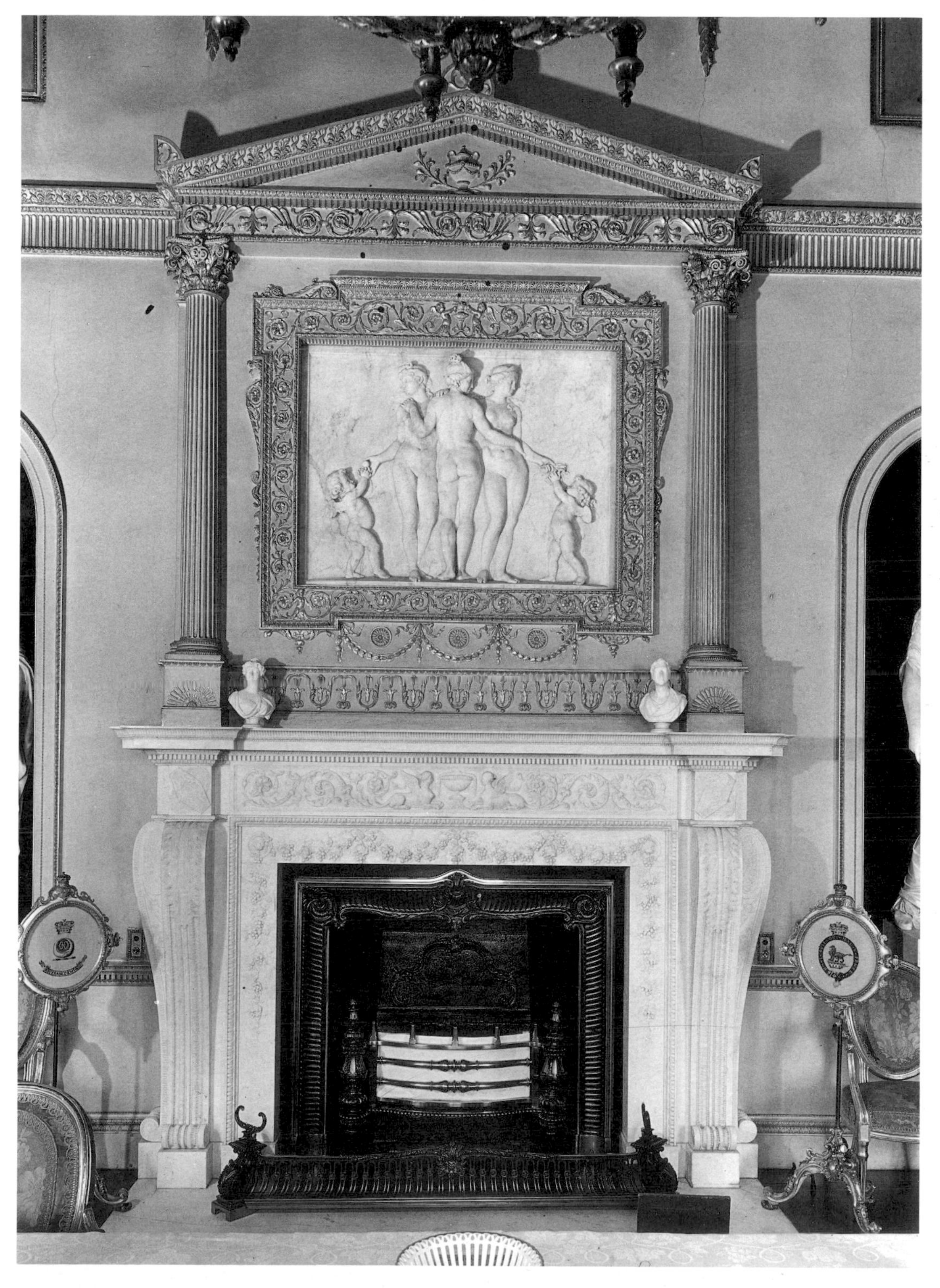

▲ ***Plate 52*** *Syon House, Brentford, Dining Room, chimney piece and overmantel with marble relief of the Three Graces. (Royal Commission on the Historical Monuments of England)*

▲ **Plate 53** *Syon House, Brentford, Red Drawing Room, general view showing ceiling medallions by Cipriani and carpet designed by Adam and made in 1769. (A. F. Kersting)*

▲ **Plate 54** *Syon House, Brentford, Red Drawing Room, white marble chimney piece with ormolu decoration by Matthew Boulton. (Royal Commission on the Historical Monuments of England)*

▲ ***Plate 55*** *Syon House, Brentford, Red Drawing Room, doorway: the pilasters are decorated with ormolu on an ivory background. (A. F. Kersting)*

▲ ***Plate 56*** *Syon House, Brentford, Long Gallery, detail with portrait medallion of Hugh Smithson, lst Duke of Northumberland, 1766: the pilasters, – of which there are 62, painted by Michelangelo Pergolesi. (Royal Commission on the Historical Monuments of England)*

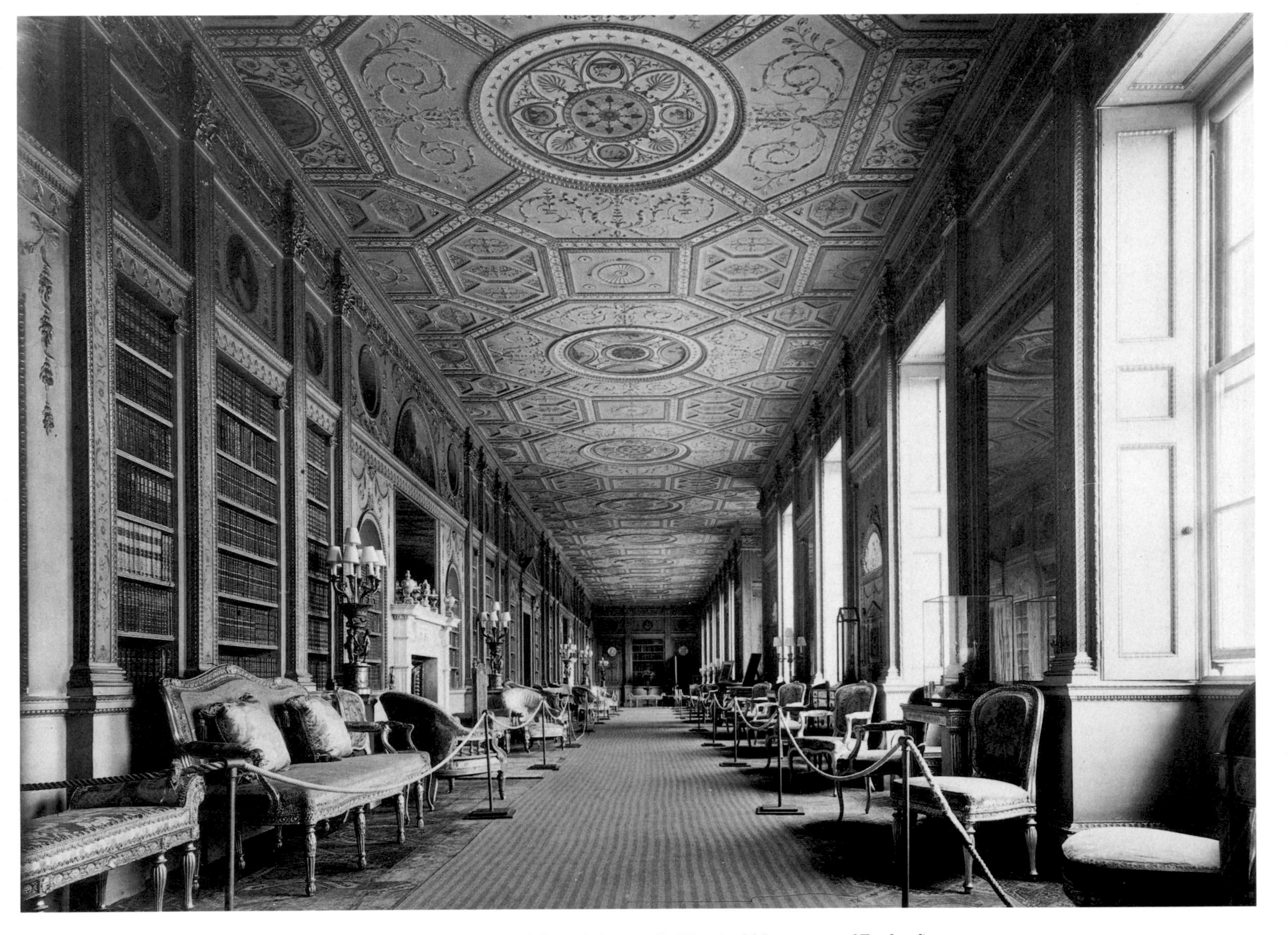

▲ **Plate 57** *Syon House, Brentford, Long Gallery, general view. (Royal Commission on the Historical Monuments of England)*

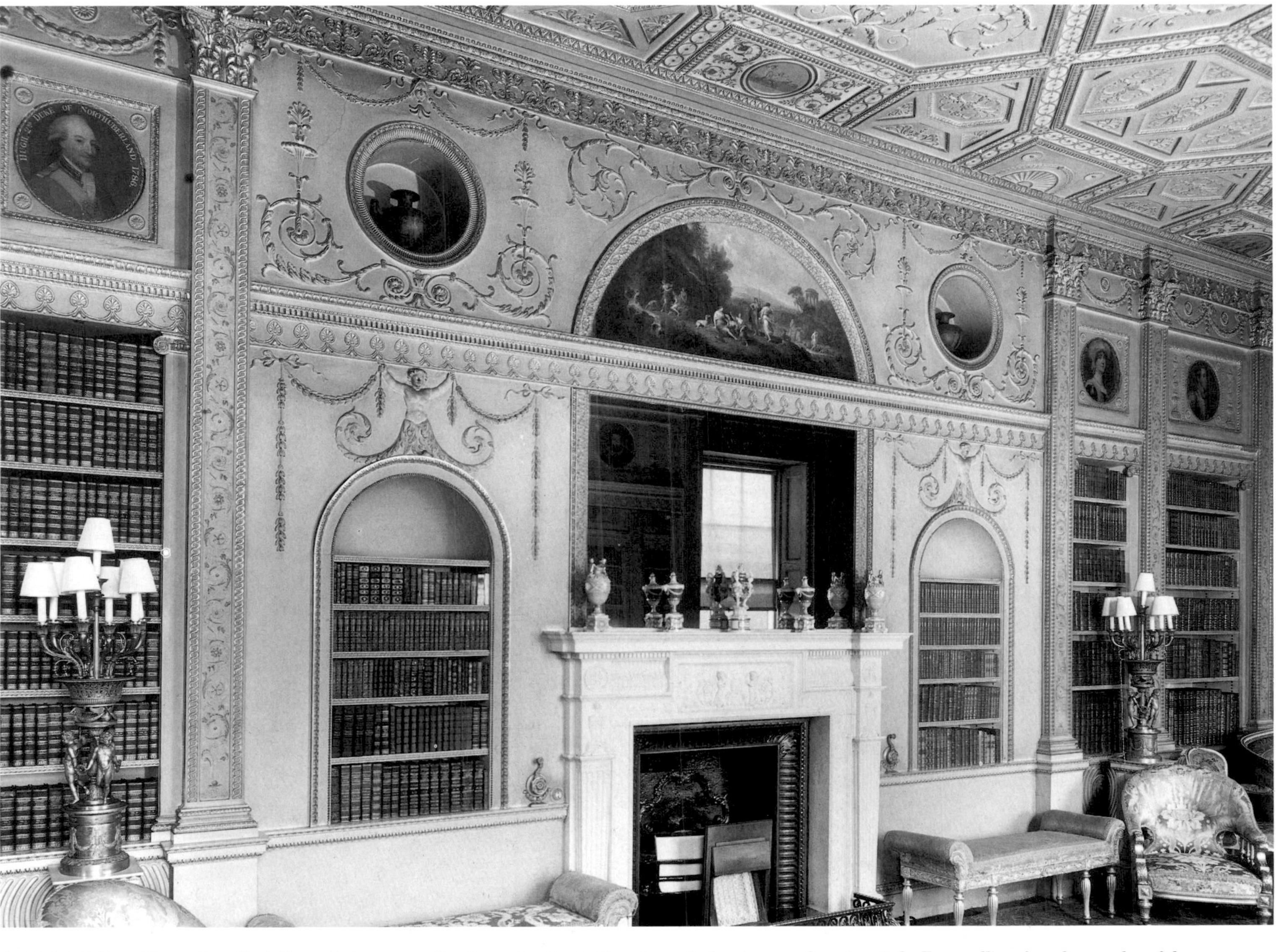

▲ **Plate 58** *Syon House, Brentford, Long Gallery, one of the two tripartite fireplace bays: the lunette over the mirror is by Zuccarelli, a founder member of the Royal Academy. (Royal Commission on the Historical Monuments of England)*

▲ **Plate 59** *Syon House, Brentford, Long Gallery, tripartite bay with doorway to the Duke's private appartments: above the book-cases are two classical landscapes by Thomas Marlow. (Royal Commission on the Historical Monuments of England)*

▲ **Plate 60** *Syon House, Brentford, Long Gallery, west wall with concealed doors to the cabinet, on left, and the stairs to the garden, centre. (Royal Commission on the Historical Monuments of England)*

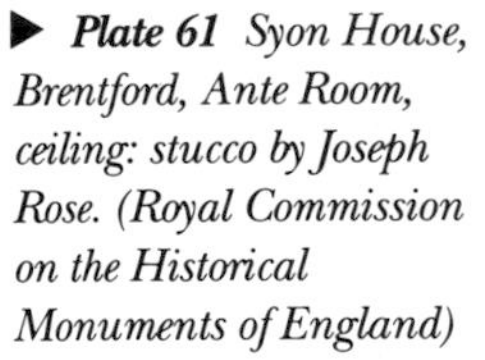

▶ **Plate 61** *Syon House, Brentford, Ante Room, ceiling: stucco by Joseph Rose. (Royal Commission on the Historical Monuments of England)*

▲ **Plate 62** *Syon House, Brentford, Private Drawing Room, marble fireplace with inlaid decoration: the grate behind the electric fire is also by Adam. (Royal Commission on the Historical Monuments of England)*

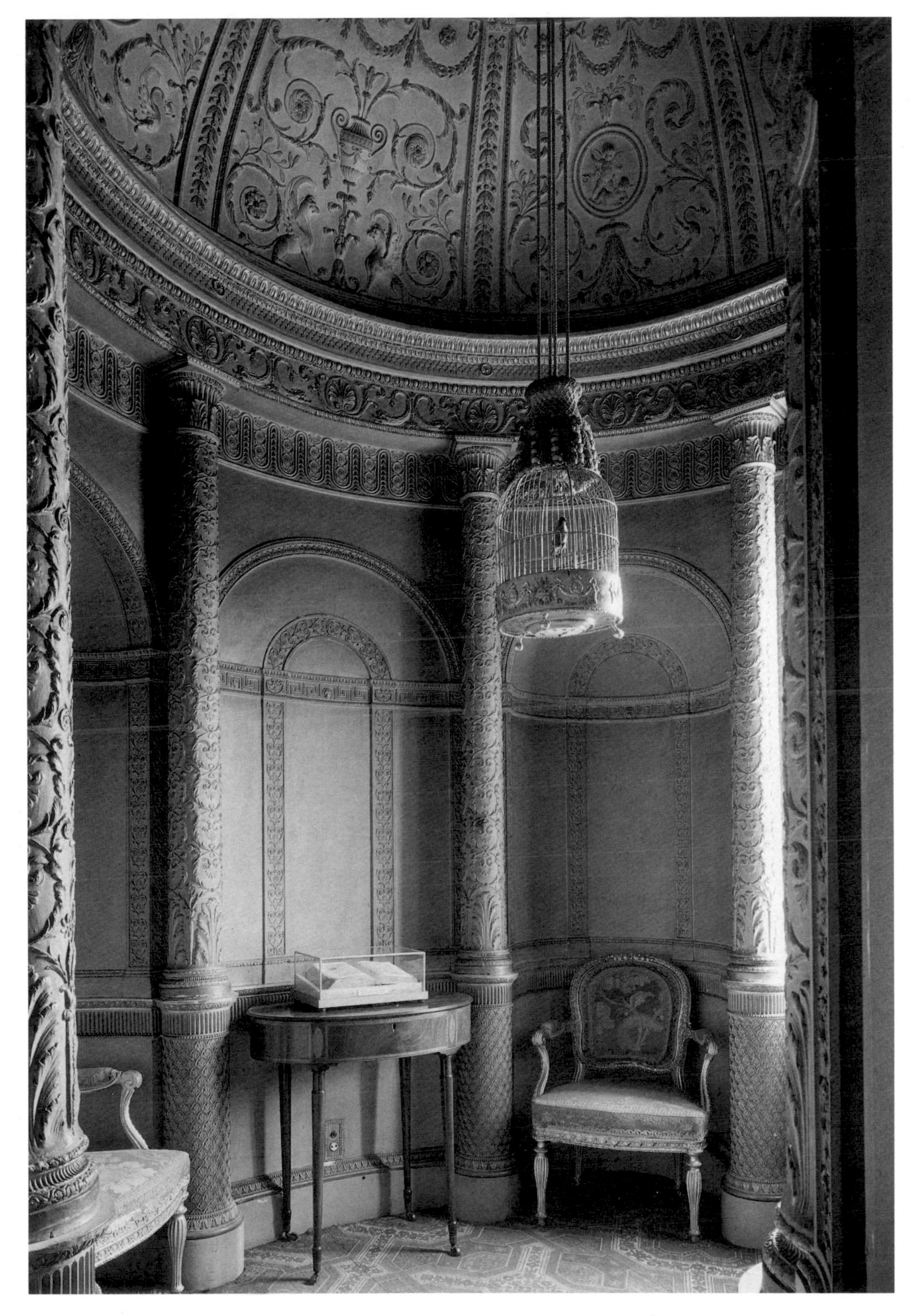

▲ ***Plate 63*** *Syon House, Brentford, circular cabinet at the east end of the Long Gallery. (Royal Commission on the Historical Monuments of England)*

▲ **Plate 64** *Syon House, Brentford, layout design for chimney piece and overmantel for the Drawing Room, 1765.*
(The Trustees of Sir John Soane's Museum)

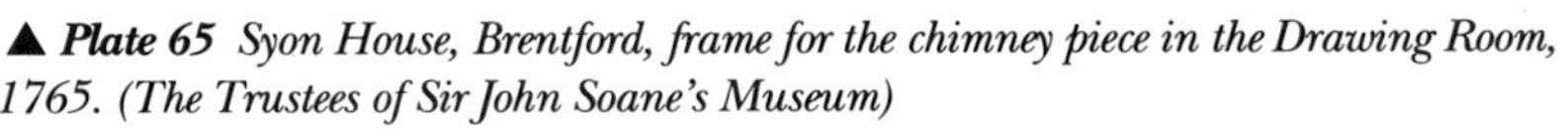

▲ **Plate 65** *Syon House, Brentford, frame for the chimney piece in the Drawing Room, 1765. (The Trustees of Sir John Soane's Museum)*

▲ **Plate 66** *Syon House, Brentford, design for a table for the (Red) Drawing Room, 1765. (The Trustees of Sir John Soane's Museum)*

▲ ***Plate 67*** *Syon House, Brentford, design for the chimney piece for the (Red) Drawing Room, 1762. (The Trustees of Sir John Soane's Museum)*

▲ ***Plate 68*** *Syon House, Brentford, design for the chimney piece for the (Red) Drawing Room, 1762. (The Trustees of Sir John Soane's Museum)*

▲ ***Plate 69*** *Syon House, Brentford, design for the chimney piece for the (Red) Drawing Room, 1762. (The Trustees of Sir John Soane's Museum)*

▲ ***Plate 70*** *Syon House, Brentford, design for the chimney piece for the (Red) Drawing Room, 1762. (Sir John Soane's Museum)*

▲ ***Plate 71*** *Syon House, Brentford, design for a table for the Dining Room, 1765. (The Trustees of Sir John Soane's Museum)*

▲ ***Plate 72*** *Syon House, Brentford, design for a table for the Hall, signed Robt. Adam, Archt., 1765. (The Trustees of Sir John Soane's Museum)*

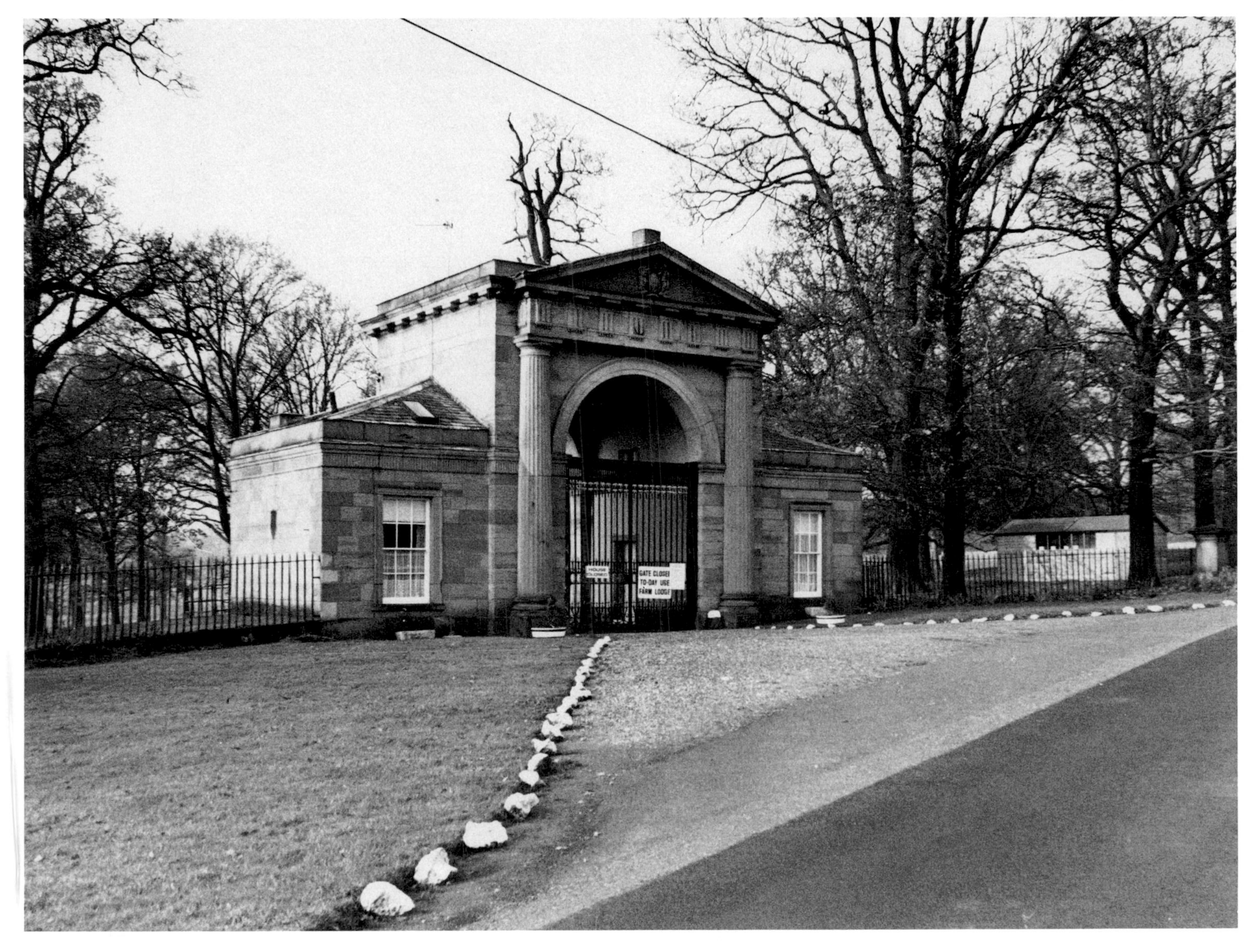

▲ **Plate 73** *Kedleston Hall, Derbyshire, North Lodge, 1760–2.*(Derby Evening Telegraph)

▶ ***Plate 74*** *Kedleston Hall, Derbyshire, Fishing House, built 1770–2. (National Trust Photographic Library)*

▲ ***Plate 75*** *Kedleston Hall, Derbyshire, Fishing house, built 1770–2, interior with plunge bath. (National Trust Photographic Library)*

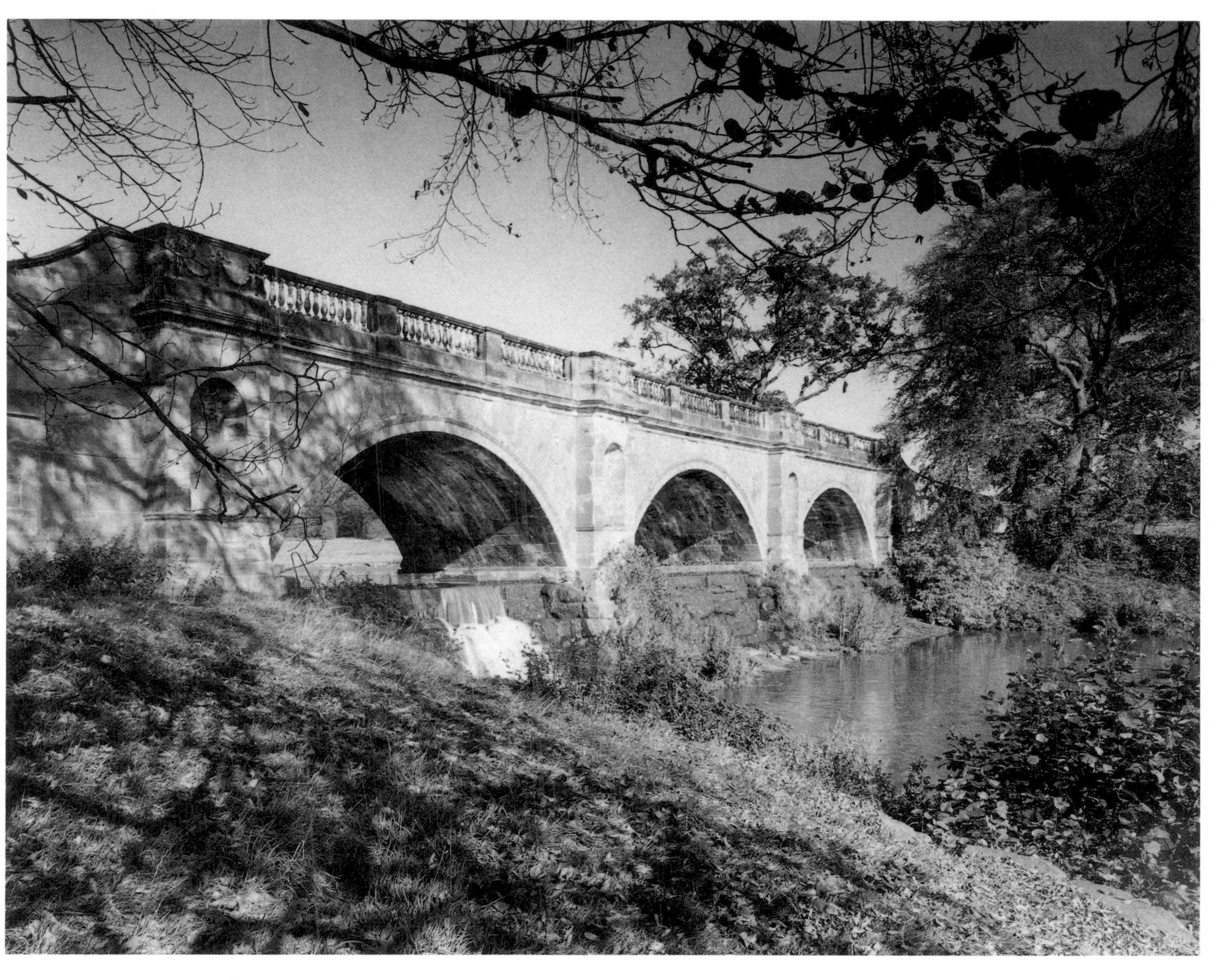

▲ **Plate 76** *Kedleston Hall, Derbyshire, cascade bridge, first design 1759, built 1770–1. (National Trust Photographic Library)*

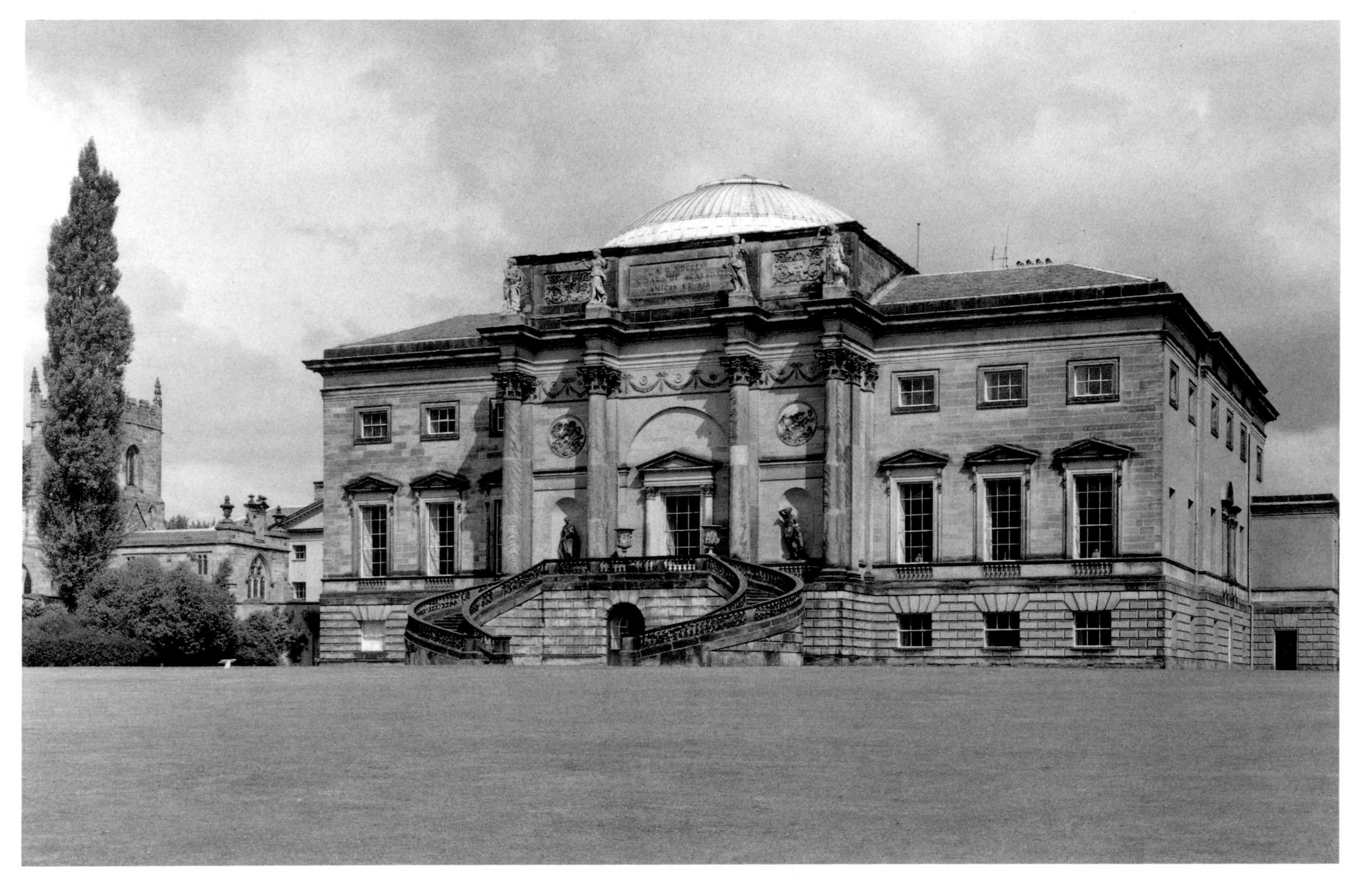

▲ **Plate 77** *Kedleston Hall, Derbyshire, 1759ff, south front, with medieval parish church to left.* (A. F. Kersting)

▲ **Plate 78** *Kedleston Hall, Derbyshire, 1759ff, Marble Hall, general view. (A. F. Kersting)*

▶ ***Plate 79*** *Kedleston Hall, Derbyshire, Marble Hall, chimney piece designed by George Richardson, 1776–7. (A. F. Kersting)*

▲ ***Plate 80*** *Kedleston Hall, Derbyshire, Drawing Room, sofa by John Linnell, 1765, based on a design by Adam of 1762. (National Trust Photographic Library)*

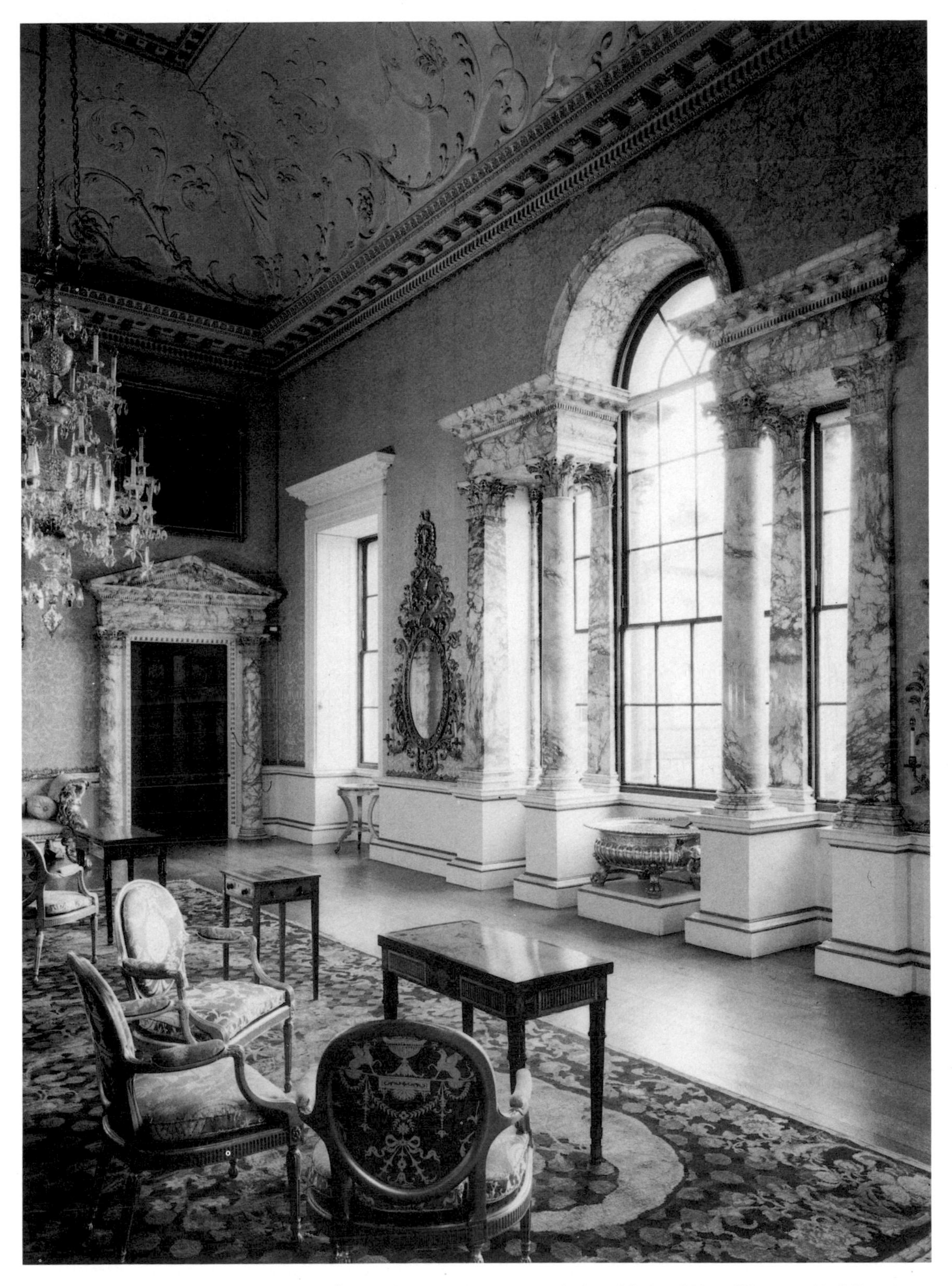

▲ **Plate 81** *Kedleston Hall, Derbyshire, 1759ff, Drawing Room, general view. (National Trust Photographic Library)*

▲ ***Plate 82*** *Kedleston Hall, Derbyshire, 1759ff, Library, general view. (National Trust Photographic Library)*

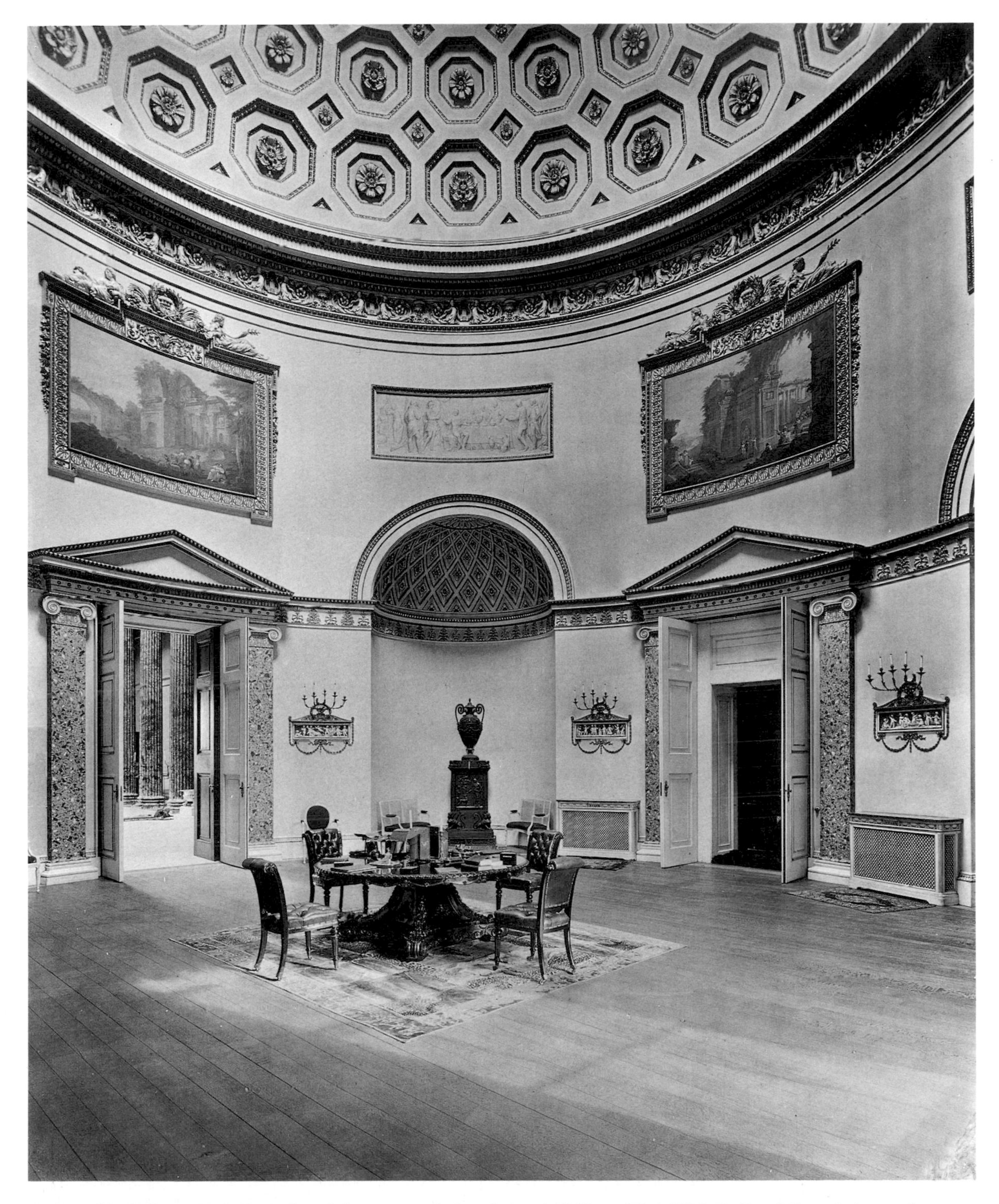

▲ ***Plate 83*** *Kedleston Hall, Derbyshire, Saloon, general view, designed 1760, modified 1788–9. (Royal Commission on the Historical Monuments of England)*

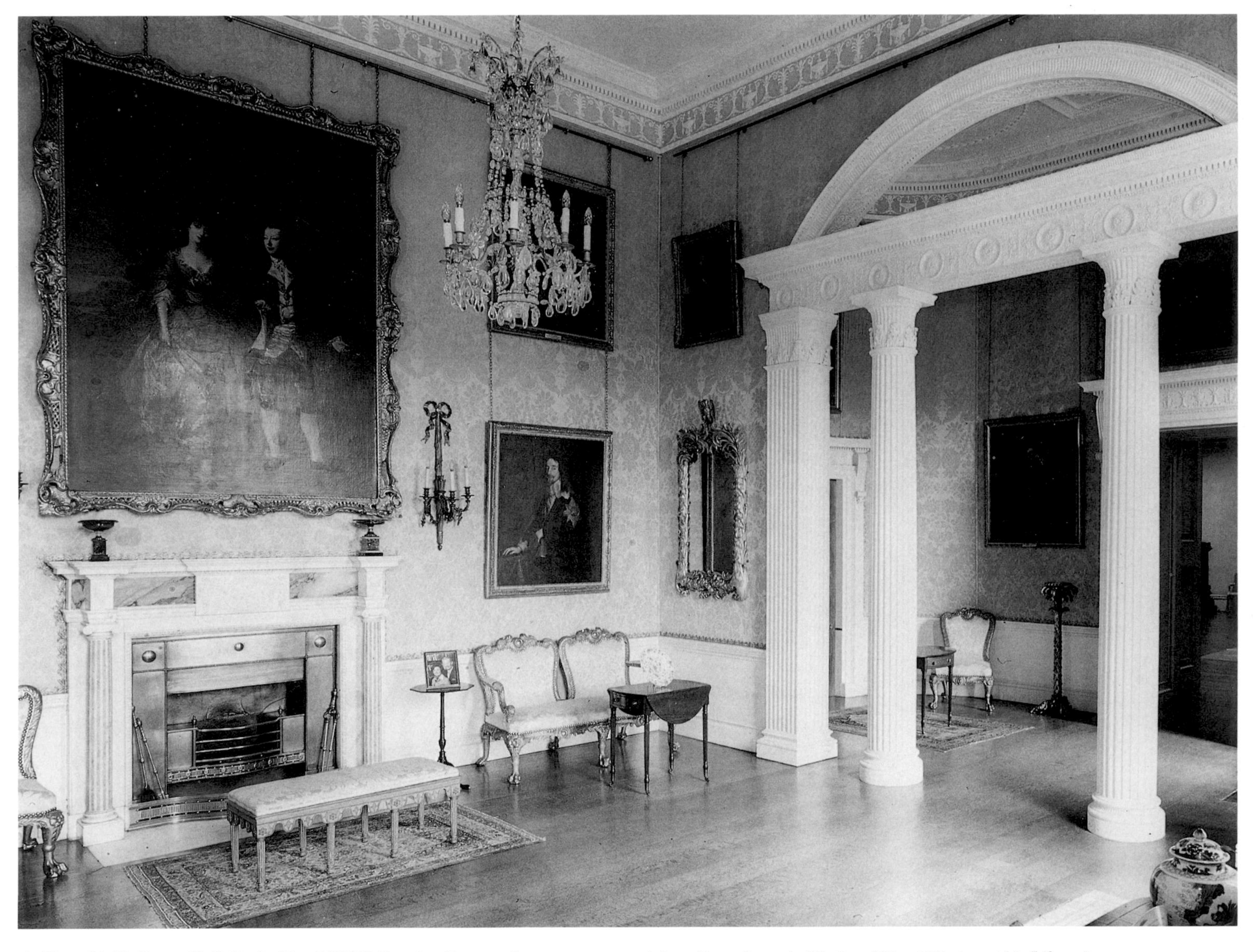

▲ ***Plate 84*** *Kedleston Hall, Derbyshire, 1759ff, Dressing Room, columnar screen and Ante Room beyond. (National Trust Photographic Library)*

▲ **Plate 85** *Kedleston Hall, Derbyshire, 1759ff, State Bedchamber and State Bed. The bed has posts in the form of palm trees, a symbol of fame, with ostrich plumes above. (National Trust Photographic Library)*

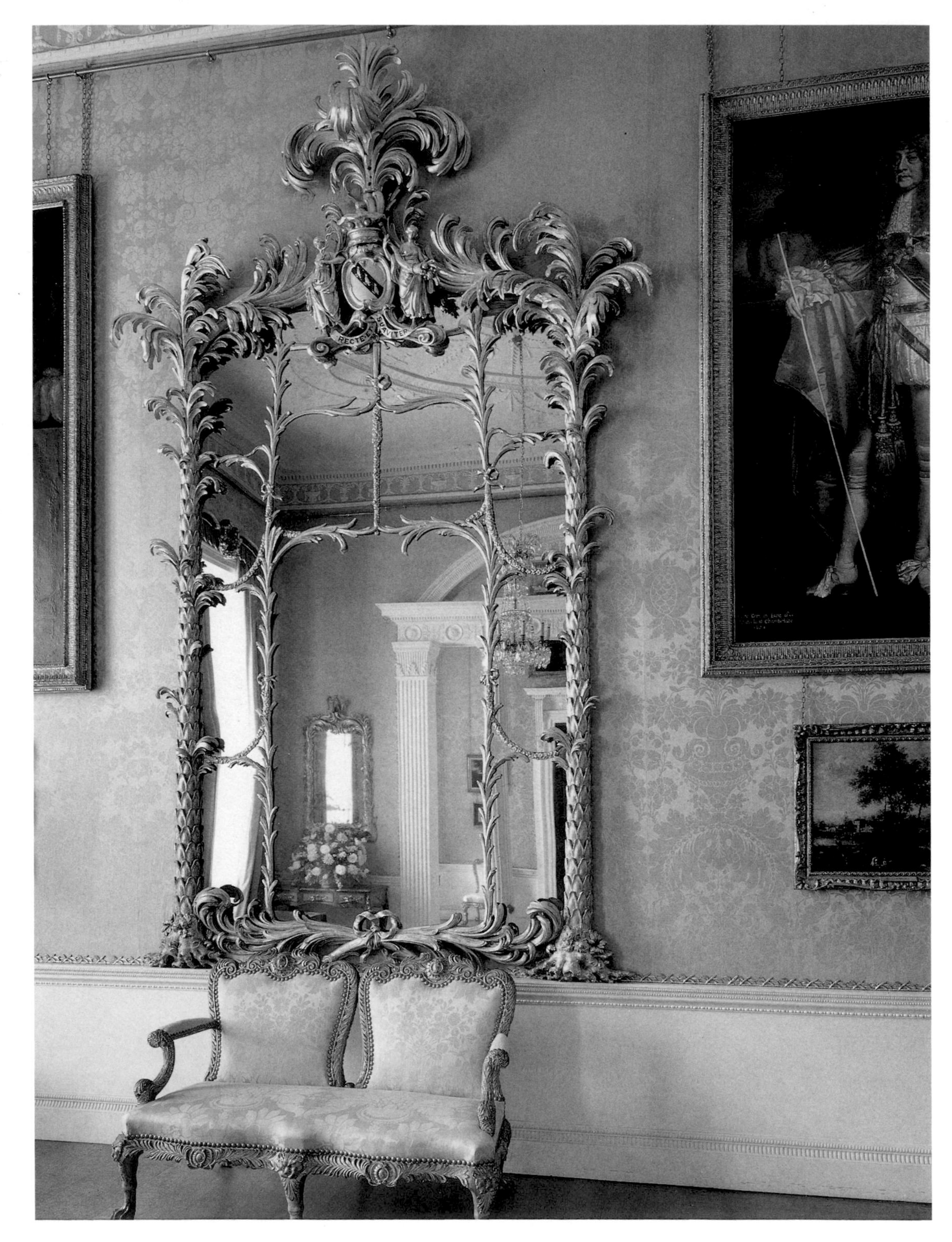

▲ ***Plate 86*** *Kedleston Hall, Derbyshire, Ante Room mirror,* c.*1768, decorated with carved gilt palm fronds. (National Trust Photographic Library)*

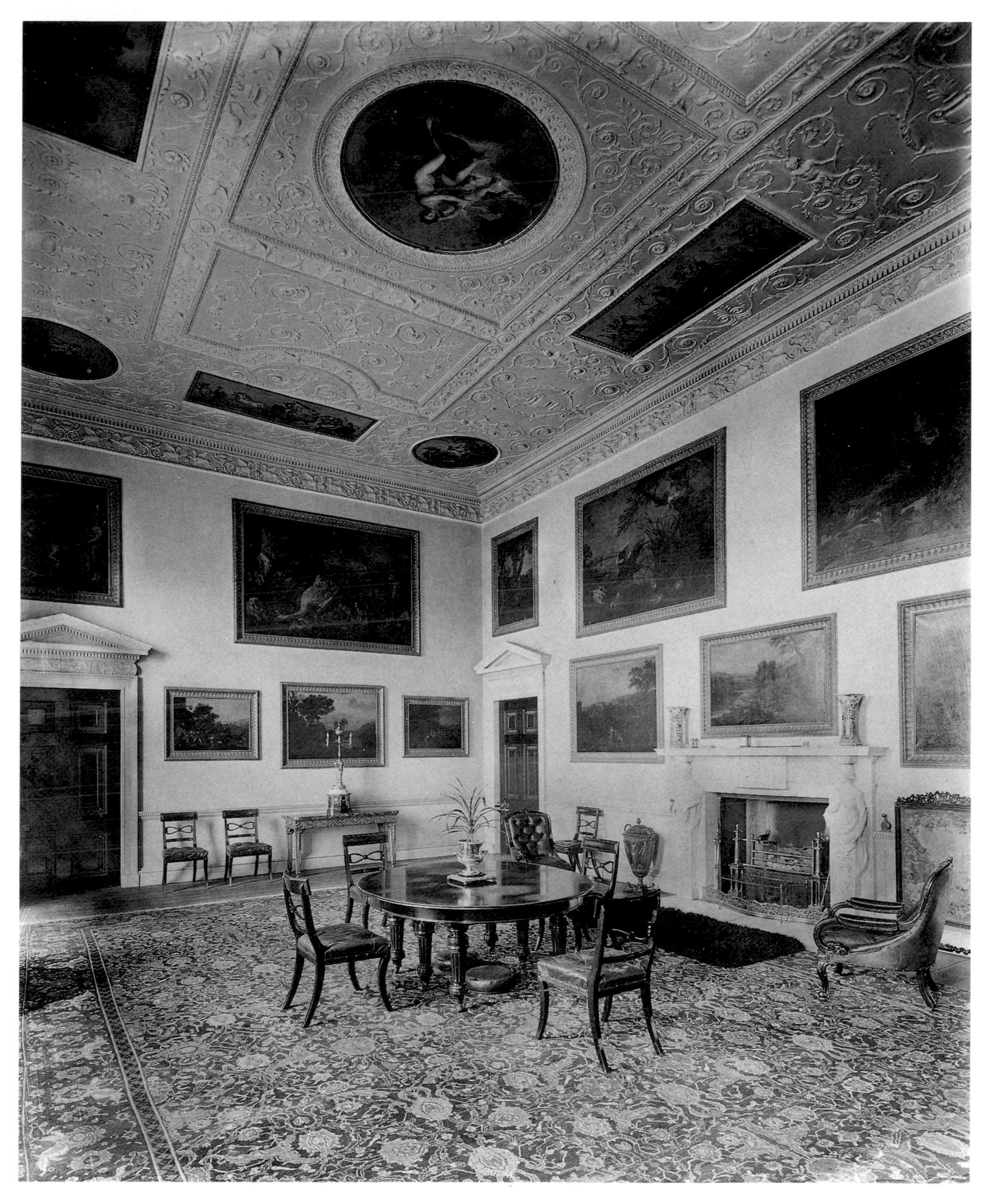

▲ ***Plate 87*** *Kedleston Hall, Derbyshire, 1759ff, Dining Room, general view. (Royal Commission on the Historical Monuments of England)*

▲ **Plate 88** *Kedleston Hall, Derbyshire, east wing (built by James Paine, 1759), kitchen, general view.* (Country Life)

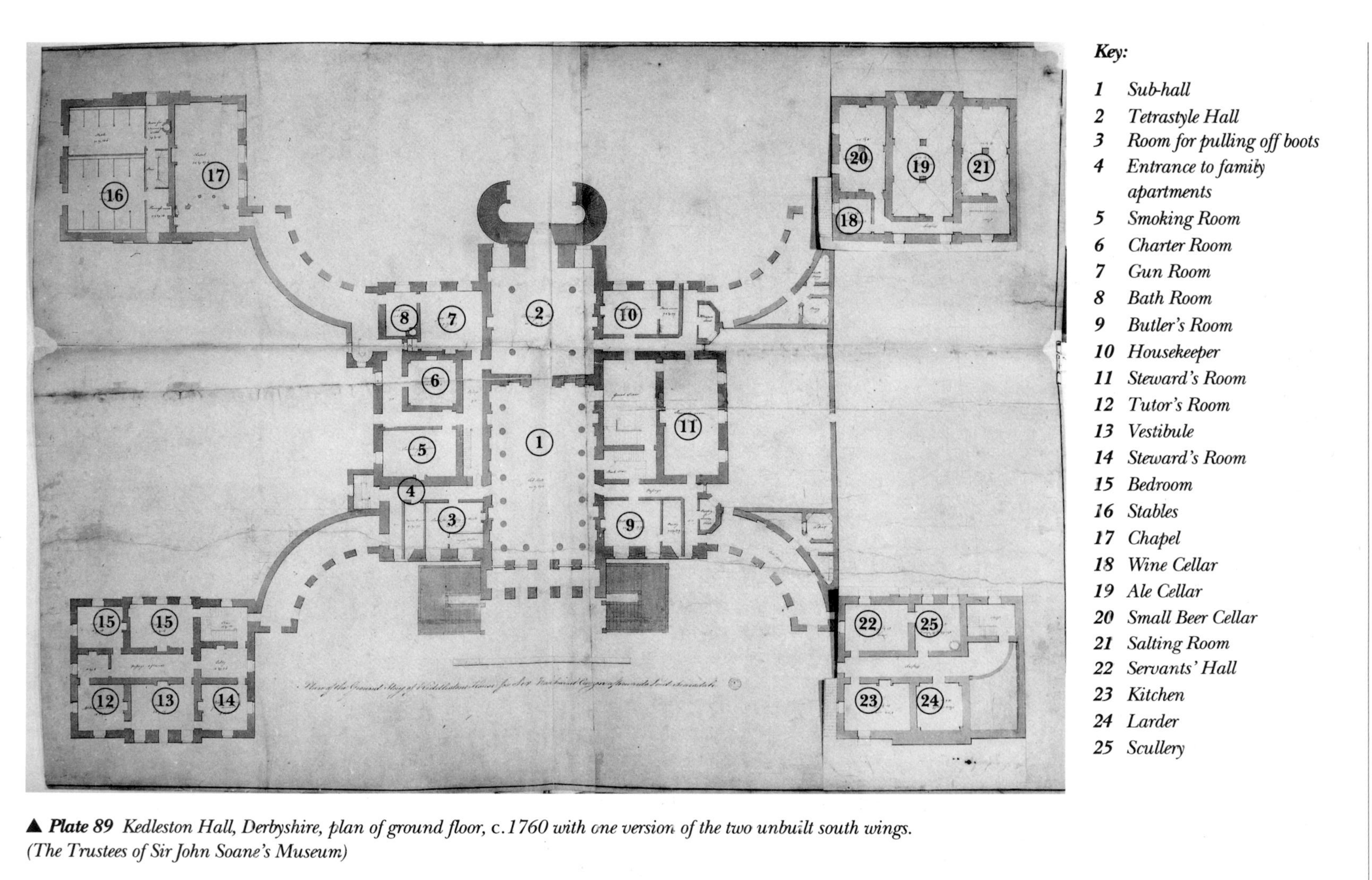

Key:

1 Sub-hall
2 Tetrastyle Hall
3 Room for pulling off boots
4 Entrance to family apartments
5 Smoking Room
6 Charter Room
7 Gun Room
8 Bath Room
9 Butler's Room
10 Housekeeper
11 Steward's Room
12 Tutor's Room
13 Vestibule
14 Steward's Room
15 Bedroom
16 Stables
17 Chapel
18 Wine Cellar
19 Ale Cellar
20 Small Beer Cellar
21 Salting Room
22 Servants' Hall
23 Kitchen
24 Larder
25 Scullery

▲ **Plate 89** *Kedleston Hall, Derbyshire, plan of ground floor,* c.1760 *with one version of the two unbuilt south wings. (The Trustees of Sir John Soane's Museum)*

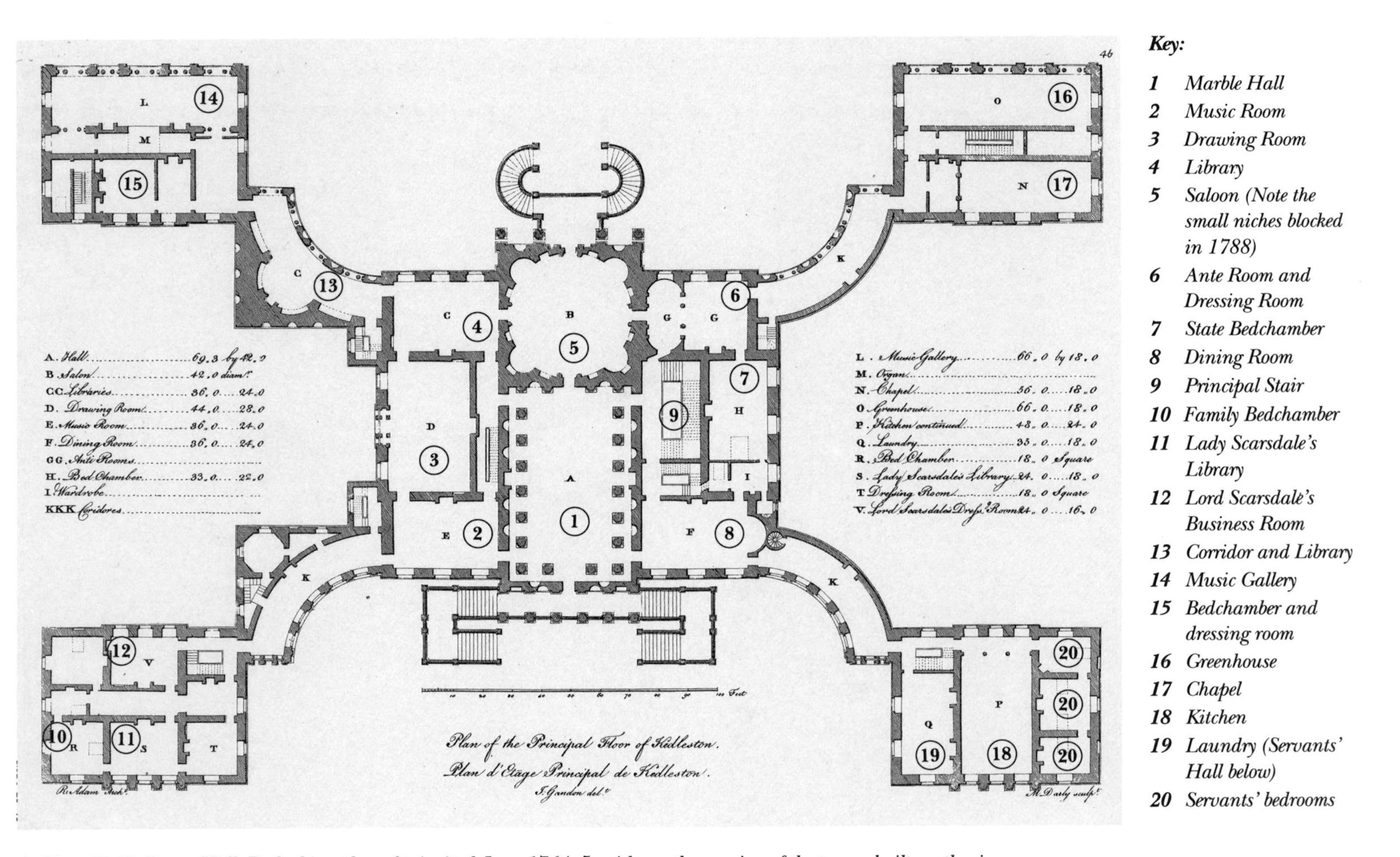

Key:

1 *Marble Hall*
2 *Music Room*
3 *Drawing Room*
4 *Library*
5 *Saloon (Note the small niches blocked in 1788)*
6 *Ante Room and Dressing Room*
7 *State Bedchamber*
8 *Dining Room*
9 *Principal Stair*
10 *Family Bedchamber*
11 *Lady Scarsdale's Library*
12 *Lord Scarsdale's Business Room*
13 *Corridor and Library*
14 *Music Gallery*
15 *Bedchamber and dressing room*
16 *Greenhouse*
17 *Chapel*
18 *Kitchen*
19 *Laundry (Servants' Hall below)*
20 *Servants' bedrooms*

▲ **Plate 90** *Kedleston Hall, Derbyshire, plan of principal floor, 1764–5, with another version of the two unbuilt south wings, and the kitchen wing as built. (National Trust Photographic Library)*

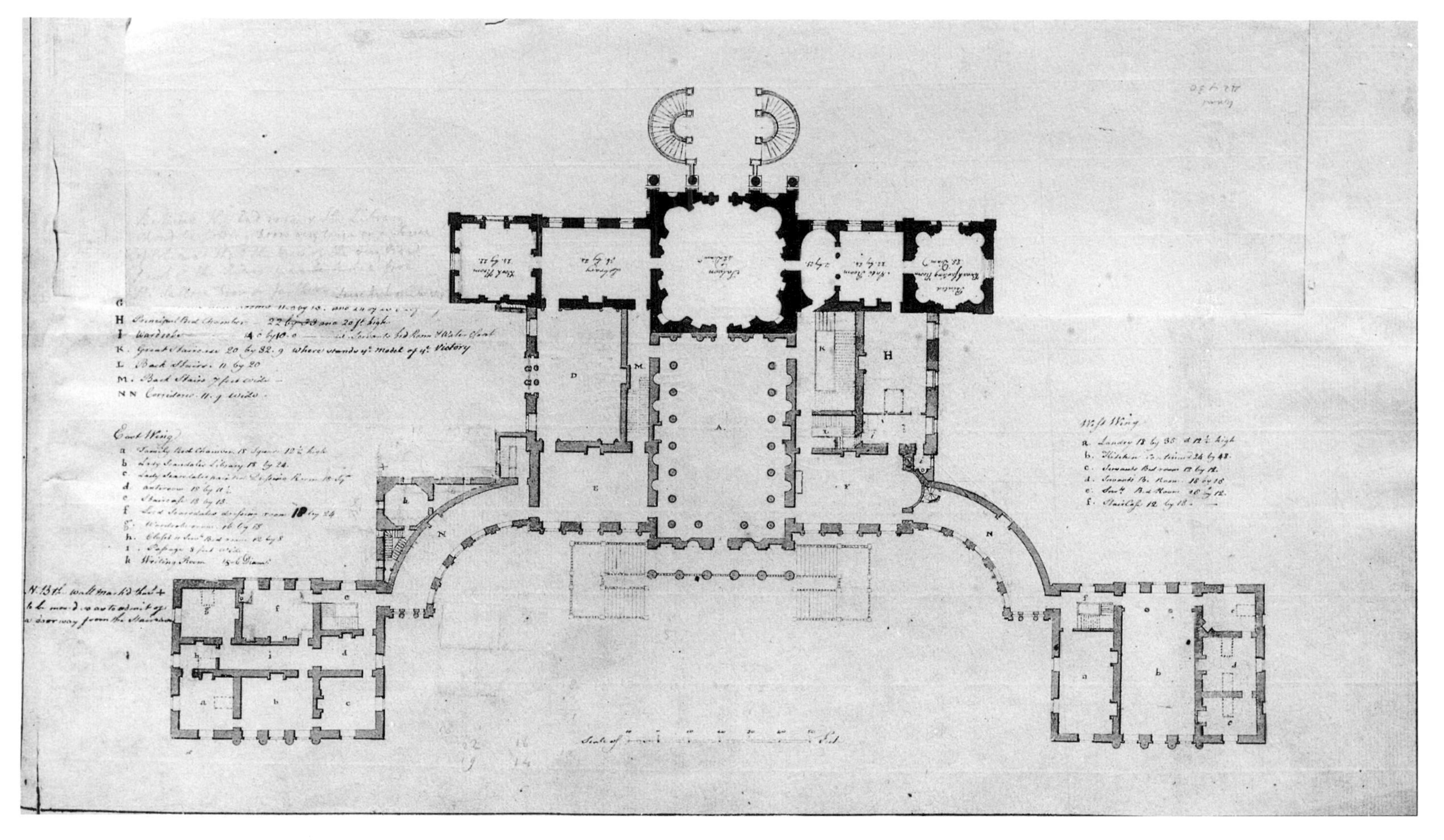

▲ **Plate 91** *Kedleston Hall, Derbyshire, 1764 plan of principal floor with overlay added 1768 showing reduced version of south front with the Book Room to the east and Painted Breakfasting Room to the west, both of which were later abandoned. (National Trust Photographic Library)*

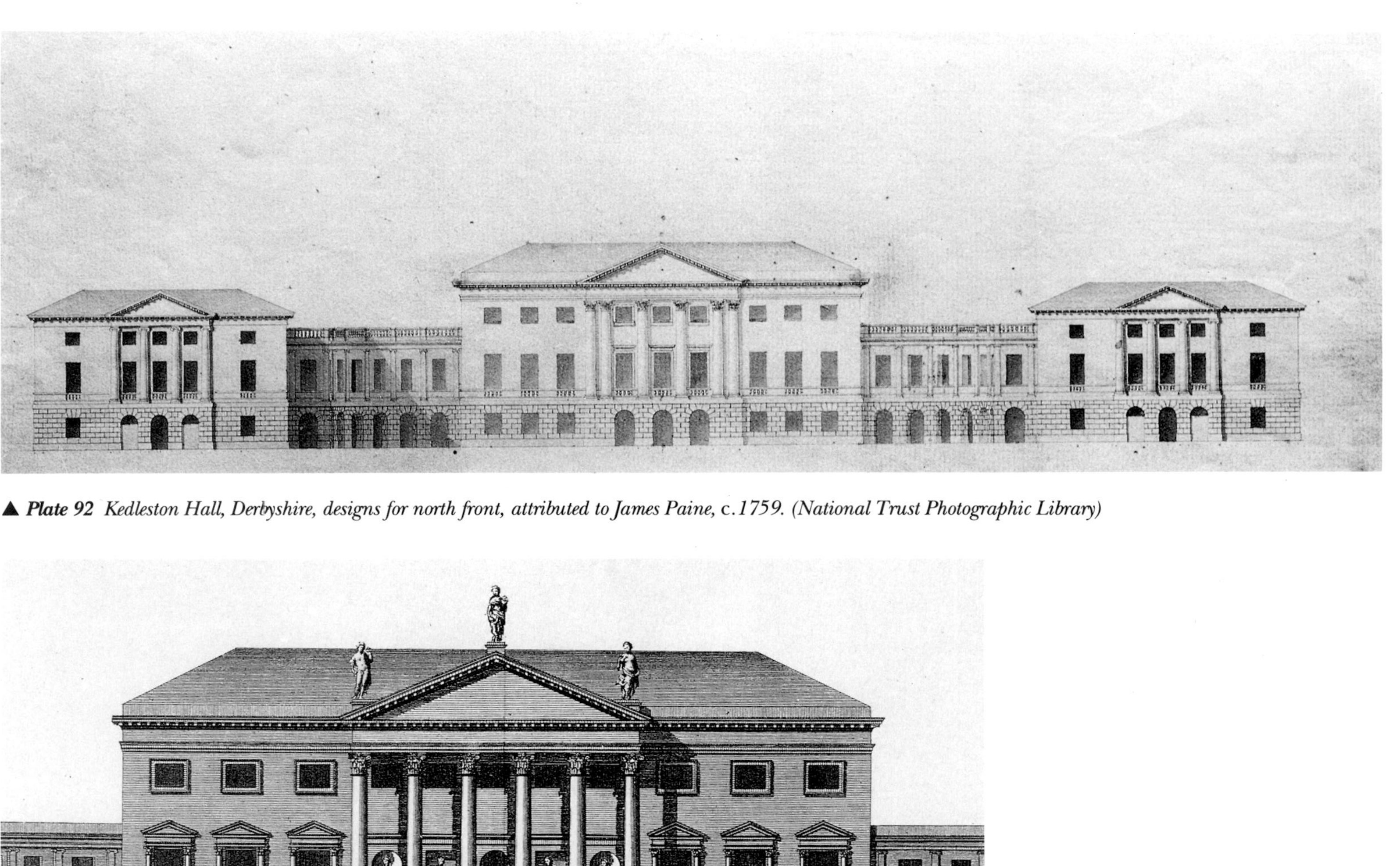

▲ **Plate 92** *Kedleston Hall, Derbyshire, designs for north front, attributed to James Paine, c.1759. (National Trust Photographic Library)*

◀ **Plate 93** *Kedleston Hall, Derbyshire, 1759ff, north front as modified by Robert Adam, reproduced from* Vitruvius Brittanicus, *Vol. IV, 1767. (Copyright: RIBA)*

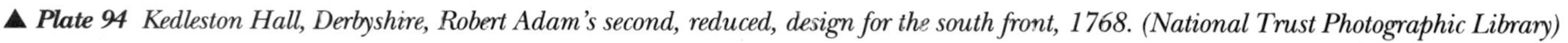

▲ **Plate 94** *Kedleston Hall, Derbyshire, Robert Adam's second, reduced, design for the south front, 1768. (National Trust Photographic Library)*

▲ **Plate 95** *Kedleston Hall, Derbyshire, cross-section of Marble Hall and Saloon, 1760. (The Trustees of Sir John Soane's Museum)*

▲ ***Plate 96*** *Kedleston Hall, Derbyshire, design for the Grand Staircase, 1764. (Note that the grand stair was designed only to rise to the piano nobile.) (National Trust Photographic Library)*

▲ **Plate 97** *Kedleston Hall, Derbyshire, design for the floor of the Marble Hall (the left-hand version of the two drawn was selected). (National Trust Photographic Library)*

◀ ***Plate 98*** *Kedleston Hall, Derbyshire, design for the west end of the Dining Room, 1762.* (Country Life)

▲ ***Plate 99*** *Kedleston Hall, Derbyshire, design for the sideboard niche in the Dining Room with tables and pedestals by Adam for displaying the family silver. (National Trust Photographic Library)*

▲ **Plate 100** *Kedleston Hall, Derbyshire, design for the ceiling of the proposed Painted Breakfasting Room, 1768. (National Trust Photographic Library)*

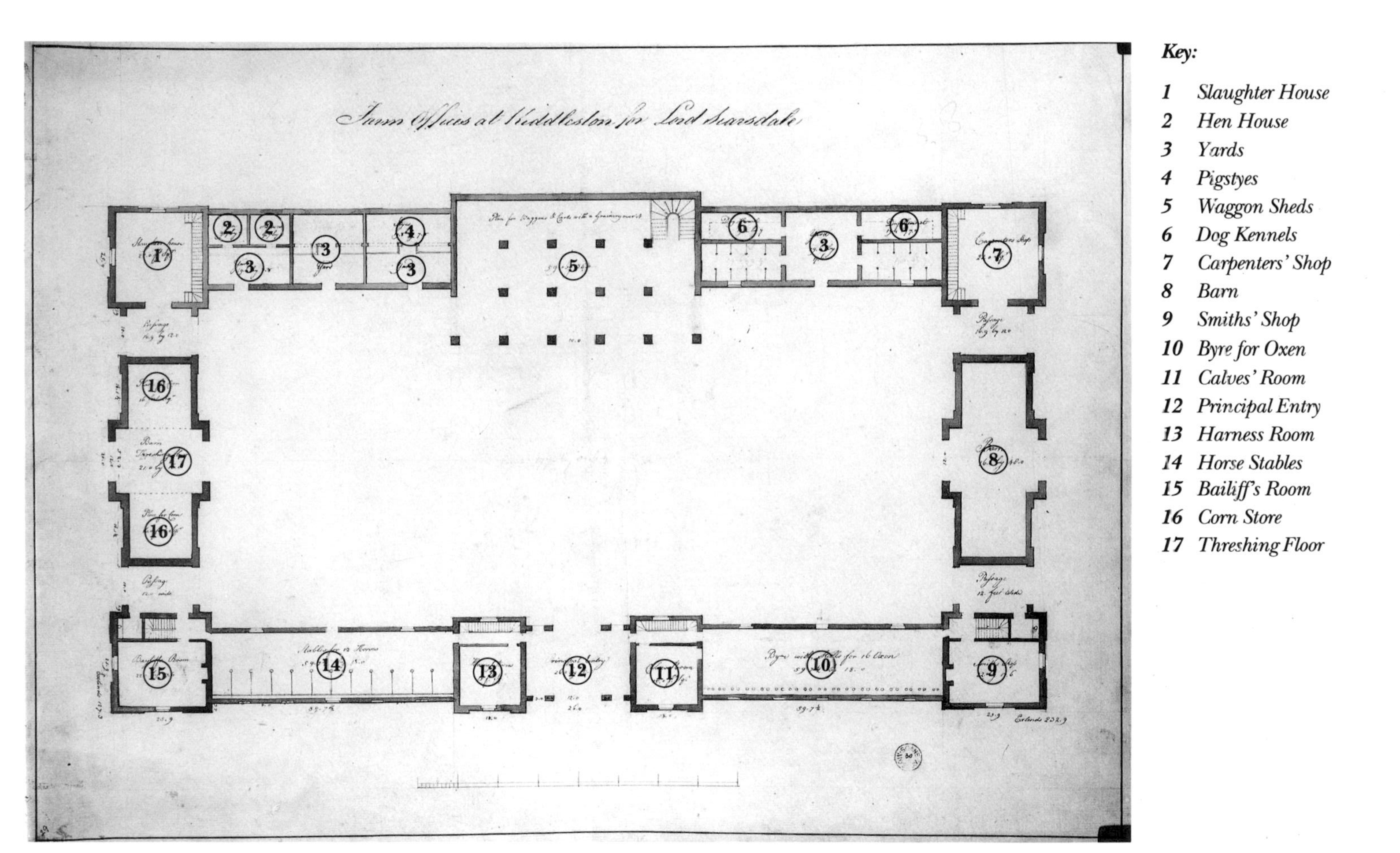

▲ **Plate 101** *Kedleston Hall, Derbyshire, plan of Farm Offices,* c.1760. *(The Trustees of Sir John Soane's Museum)*

Key:

1 *Slaughter House*
2 *Hen House*
3 *Yards*
4 *Pigstyes*
5 *Waggon Sheds*
6 *Dog Kennels*
7 *Carpenters' Shop*
8 *Barn*
9 *Smiths' Shop*
10 *Byre for Oxen*
11 *Calves' Room*
12 *Principal Entry*
13 *Harness Room*
14 *Horse Stables*
15 *Bailiff's Room*
16 *Corn Store*
17 *Threshing Floor*

▲ **Plate 102** *Kedleston Hall, Derbyshire, elevation of Farm Offices,* c.*1760, built in a much modified form. (The Trustees of Sir John Soane's Museum)*

▲ **Plate 103** *Kedleston Hall, Derbyshire, design for a gothic Chapel,* c.*1759, unexecuted. (The Trustees of Sir John Soane's Museum)*

▲ ***Plate 104*** *Kedleston Hall, Derbyshire, design for a rustic cottage,* c.*1759, unexecuted. (The Trustees of Sir John Soane's Museum)*

▲ ***Plate 105*** *Kedleston Hall, Derbyshire, design for a 'Hutt for the Honble Miss Curzon at the Upper end of Garden',* c.*1759, unexecuted. (The Trustees of Sir John Soane's Museum)*

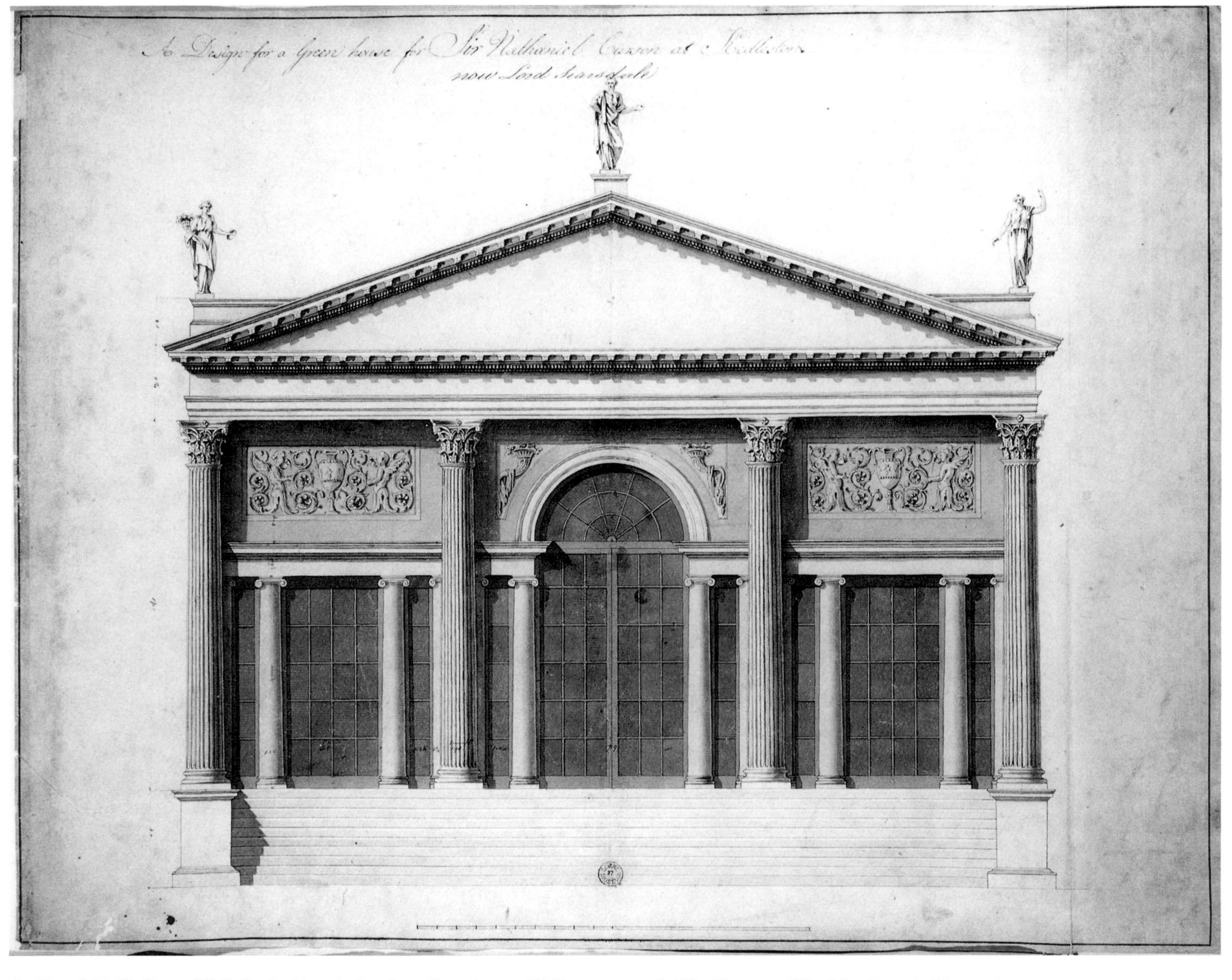

▲ **Plate 106** *Kedleston Hall, Derbyshire, design for a Greenhouse, 1749, unexecuted. (The Trustees of Sir John Soane's Museum)*

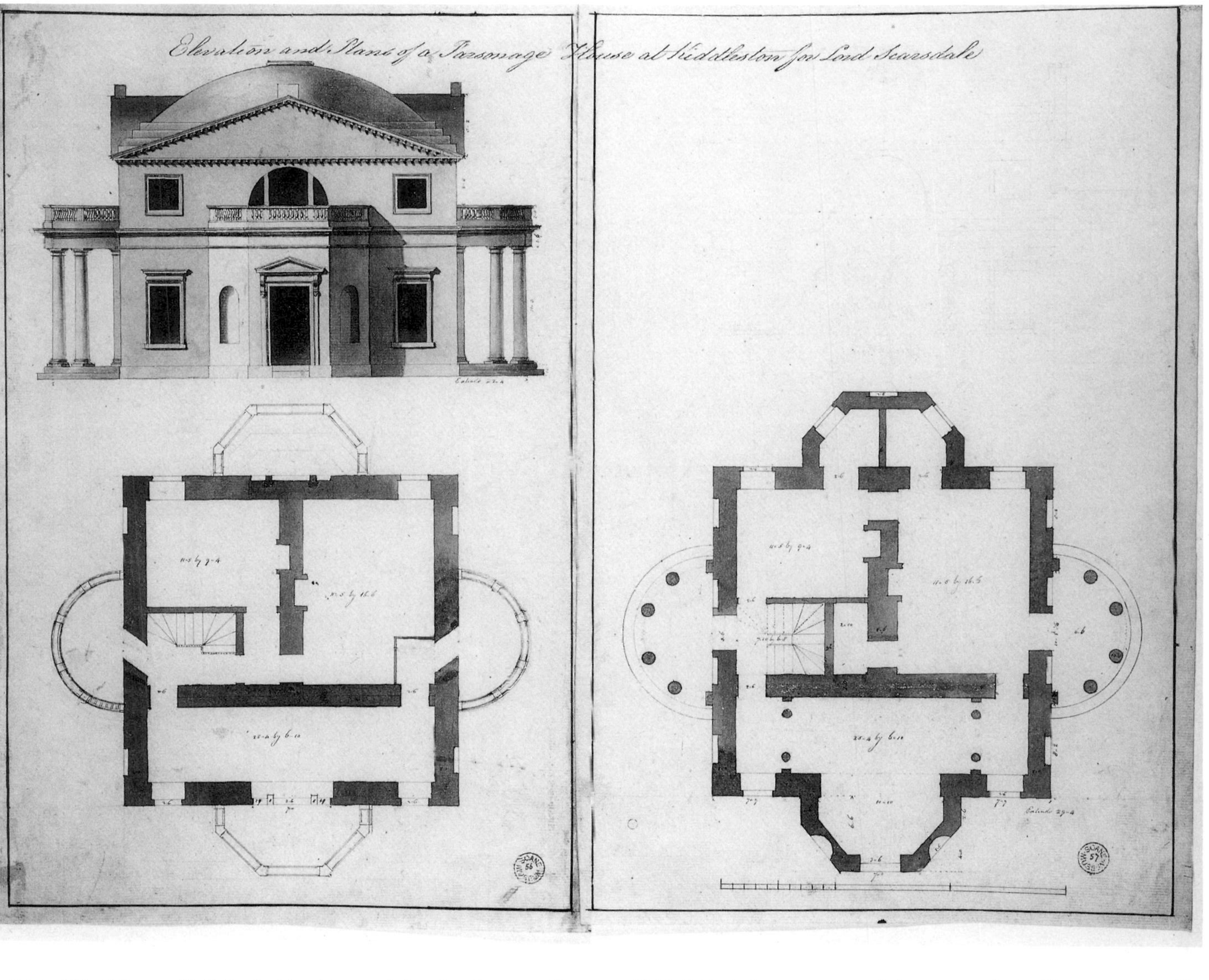

▲ **Plate 107** *Kedleston Hall, Derbyshire, plan and elevation for a new Rectory,* c.1760. *This design was not carried out, instead the old rectory was bodily removed and reconstructed. (The Trustees of Sir John Soane's Museum)*

▲ ***Plate 108*** *Kedleston Hall, Derbyshire, design for a tower 84ft high for viewing the park, 1760, unexecuted). (The Trustees of Sir John Soane's Museum)*

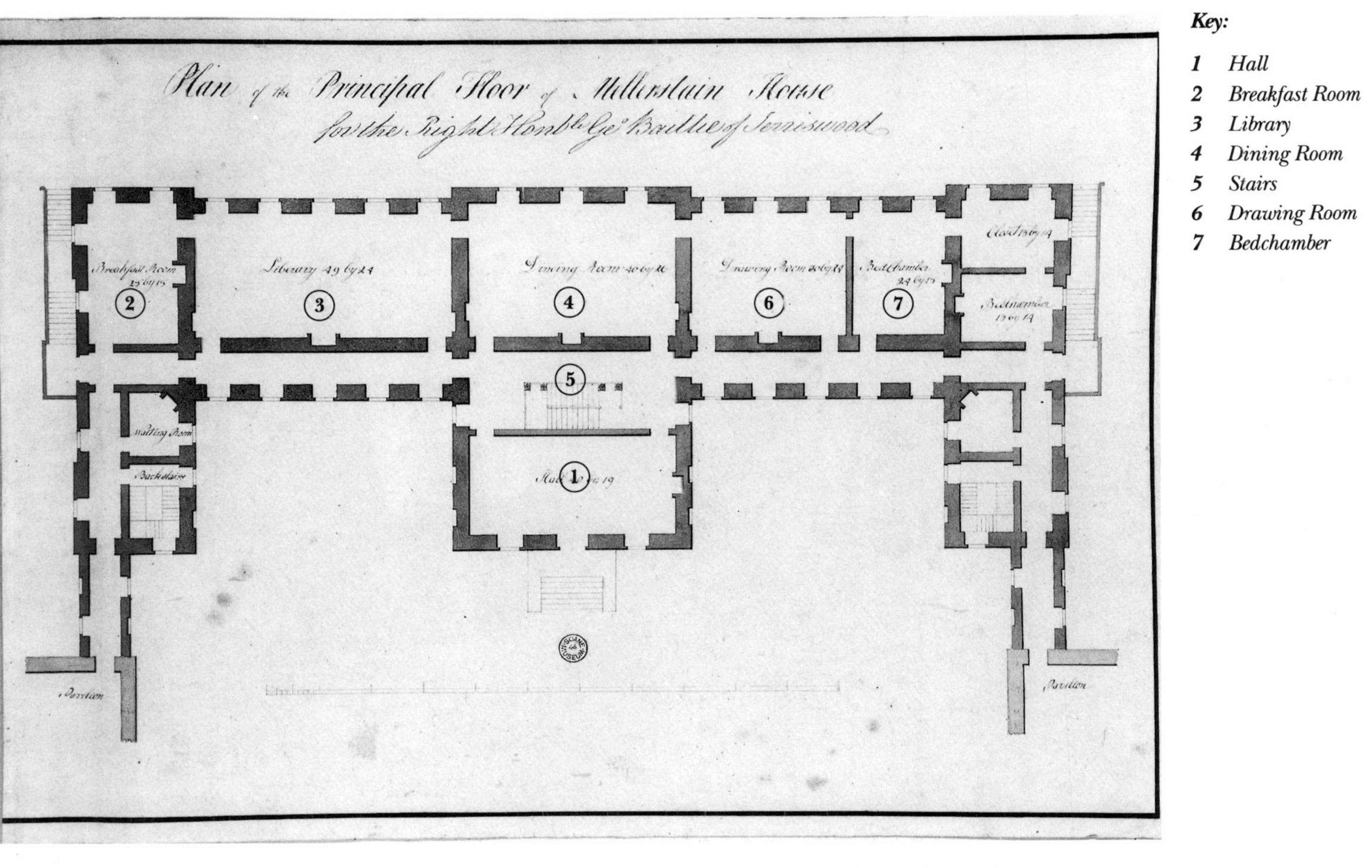

▲ **Plate 109** *Mellerstain, Berwickshire. Plan of the principal floor,* c.1770. *(The Trustees of Sir John Soane's Museum)*

Key:

1 Hall
2 Breakfast Room
3 Library
4 Dining Room
5 Stairs
6 Drawing Room
7 Bedchamber

▲ **Plate 110** *Mellerstain, Berwickshire,* c.*1770–8, north front. (A. F. Kersting)*

▲ **Plate 111** *Mellerstain, Berwickshire, south front. (A. F. Kersting)*

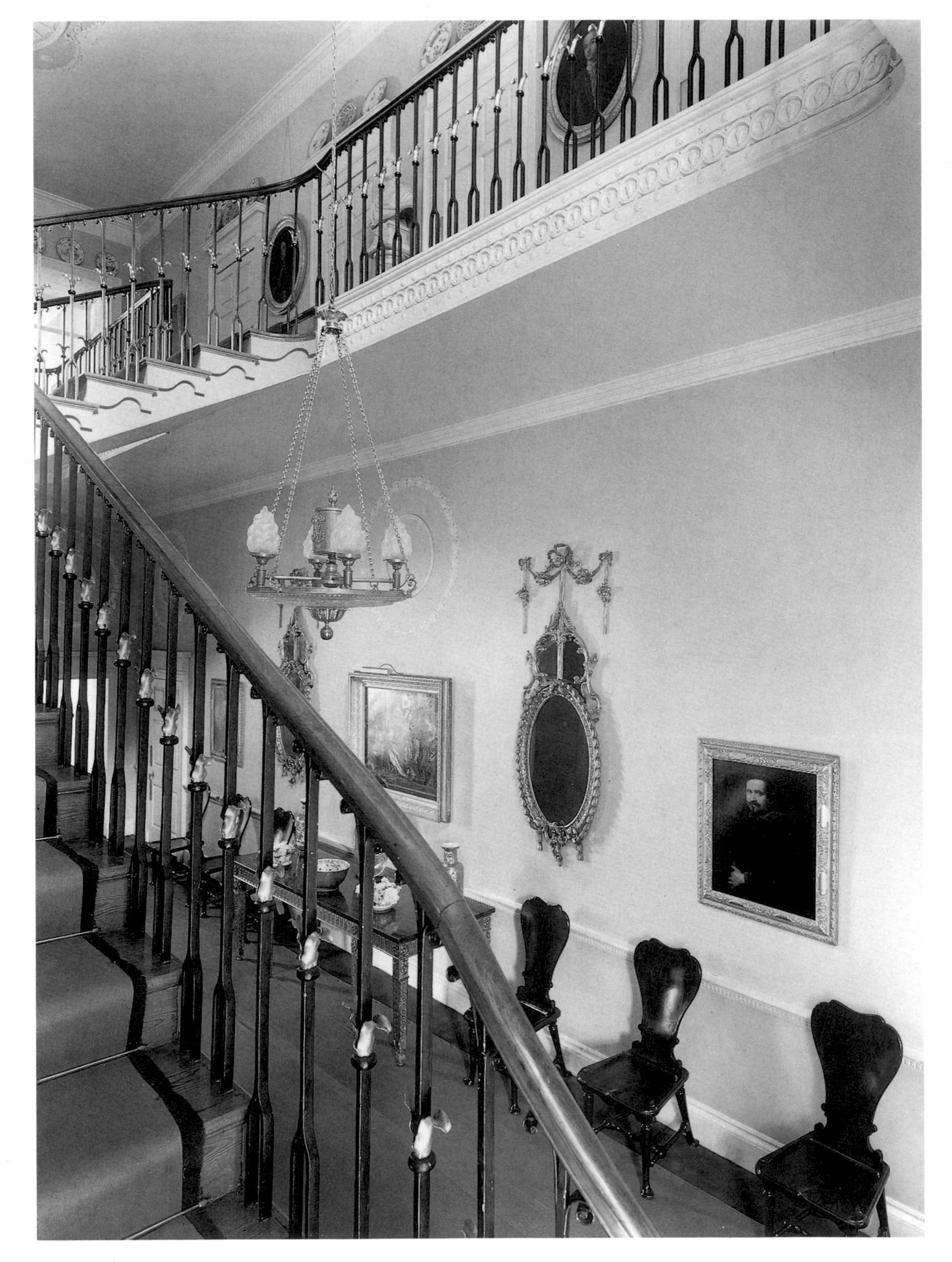

▲ ***Plate 112*** *Mellerstain, Berwickshire, principal stairs. (A. F. Kersting)*

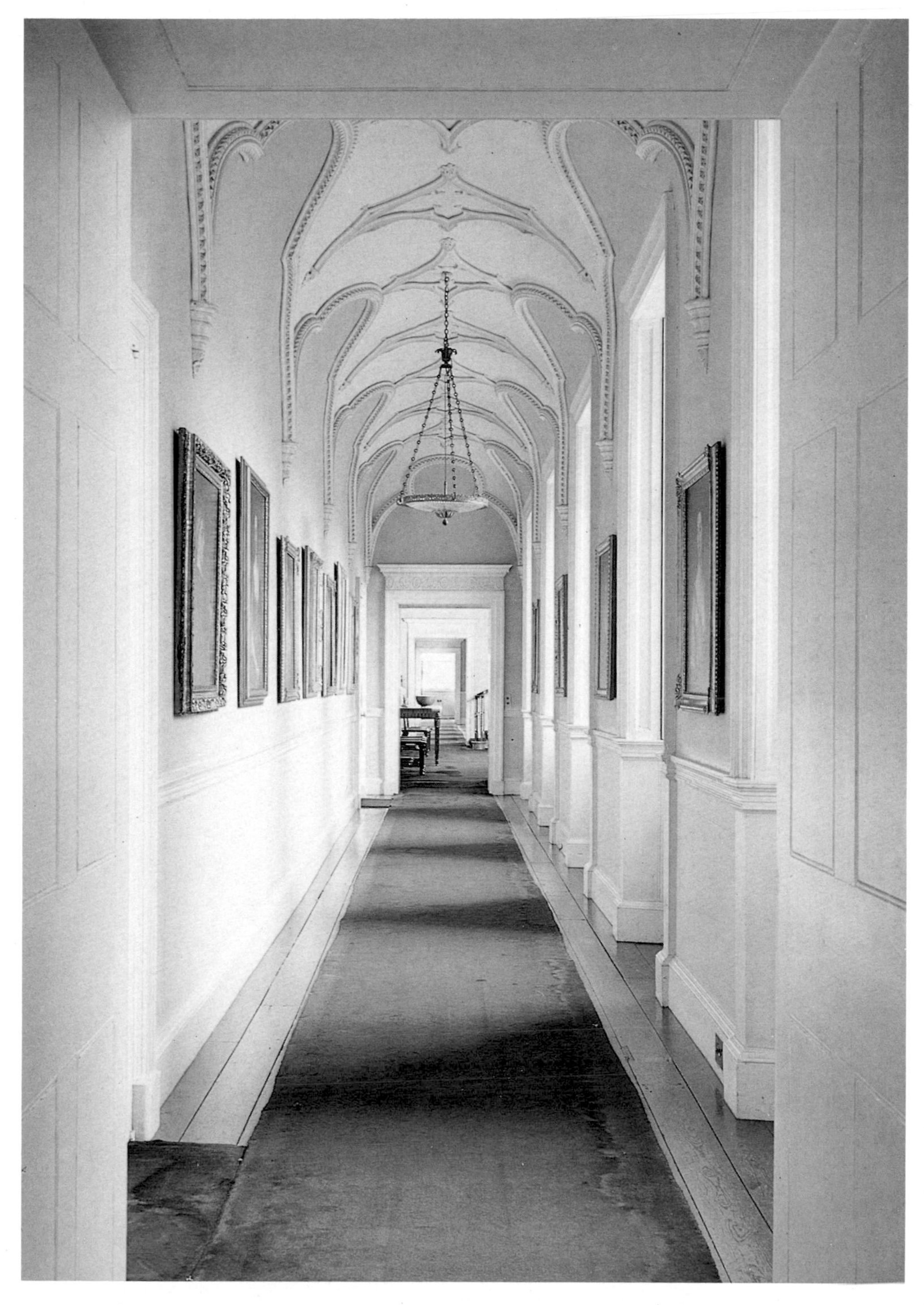

▲ ***Plate 113*** *Mellerstain, Berwickshire, west passage, with gothic pattern to vaulting ribs. (Newbery Smith Photography)*

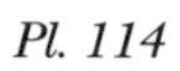

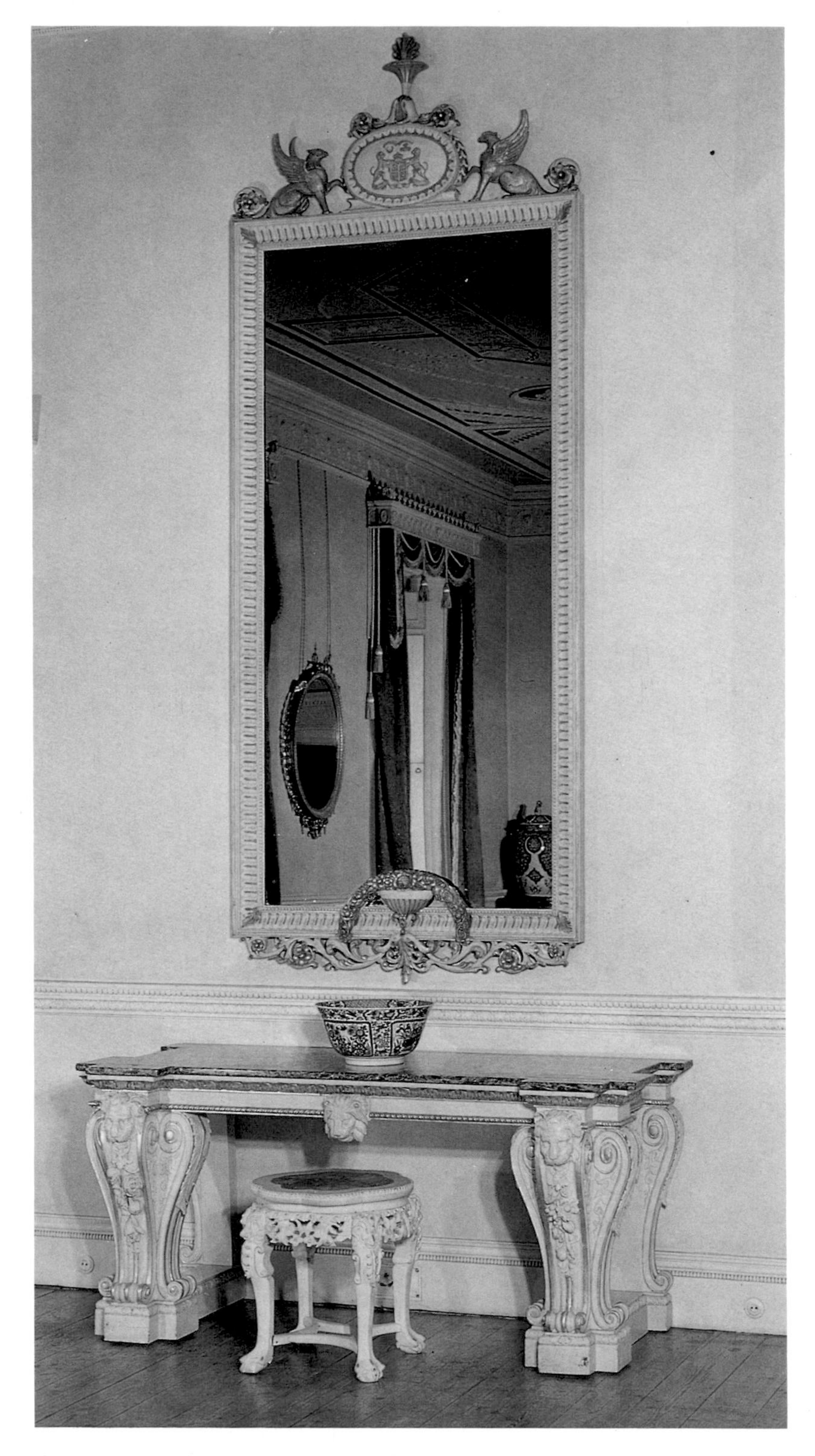

▲ ***Plate 114*** *Mellerstain, Berwickshire, Pier glass and table in the Dining Room (now called the Music Room). (Newbery Smith Photography)*

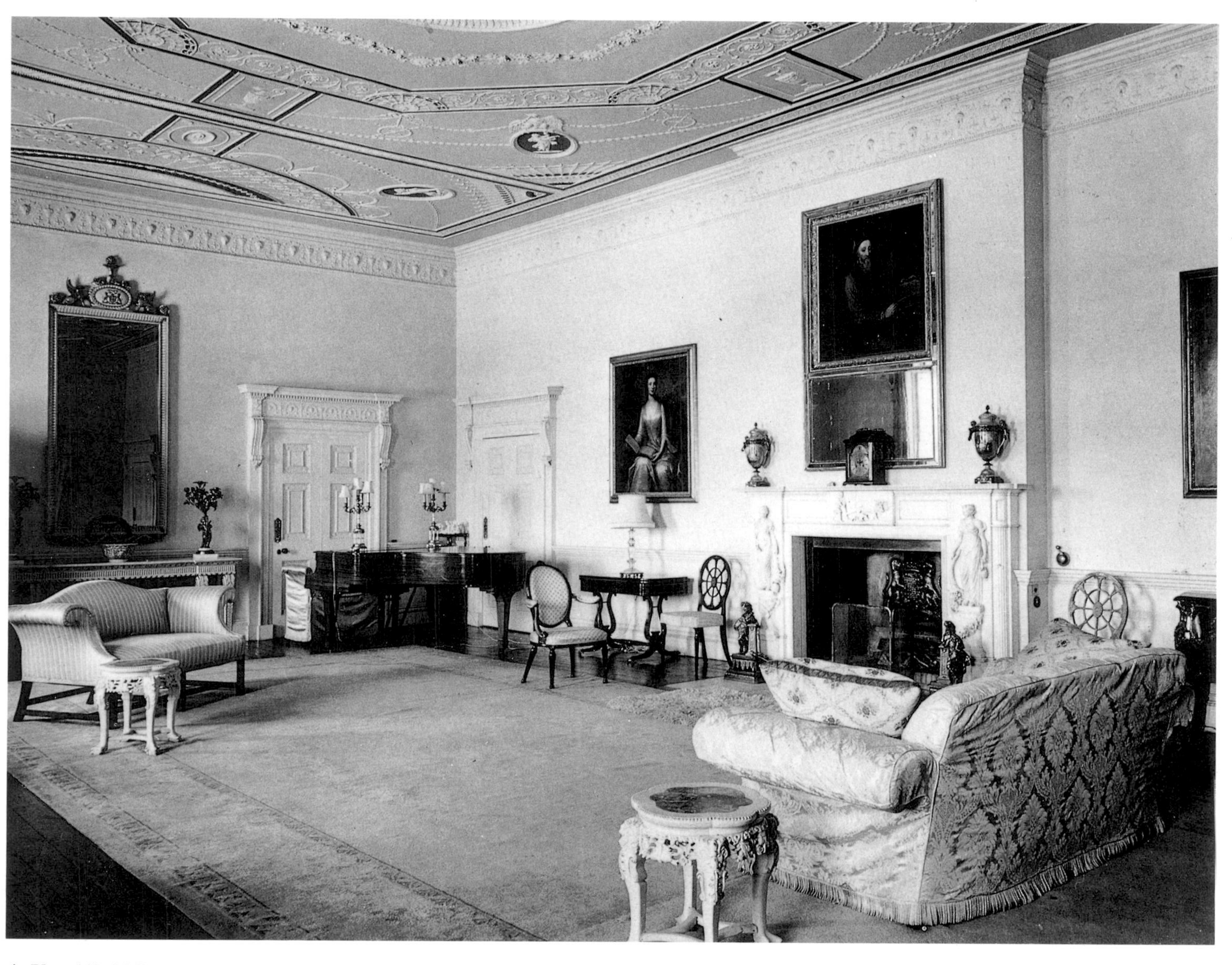

▲ ***Plate 115*** *Mellerstain, Berwickshire, Dining Room (now called the Music Room), general view looking west. (Mellerstain Trust)*

▲ **Plate 116** *Mellerstain, Berwickshire, Dining Room (now called the Music Room), general view looking east.* (A. F. Kersting)

▲ ***Plate 117*** *Mellerstain, Berwickshire, Dining Room (now called the Music Room), detail of ceiling. (A. F. Kersting)*

▲ **Plate 118** *Mellerstain, Berwickshire, Library, detail of plaster panel from the frieze – Priam begging Achilles for the body of Hector (a scene from Homer's* Iliad*). (A. F. Kersting)*

▶ **Plate 119** *Mellerstain, Berwickshire, Library, detail, portrait of Lady Grisel Baillie in 1746 at the age of 62. (She was the wife of George Baillie who commissioned William Adam in 1725 and grandmother of George Hamilton Baillie who commissioned Robert Adam.) (Mellerstain Trust)*

▲ **Plate 120** *Mellerstain, Berwickshire, Library, pier glass and cupboard. (A. F. Kersting)*

▲ **Plate 121** *Mellerstain, Berwickshire, Drawing Room, general view. (A. F. Kersting)*

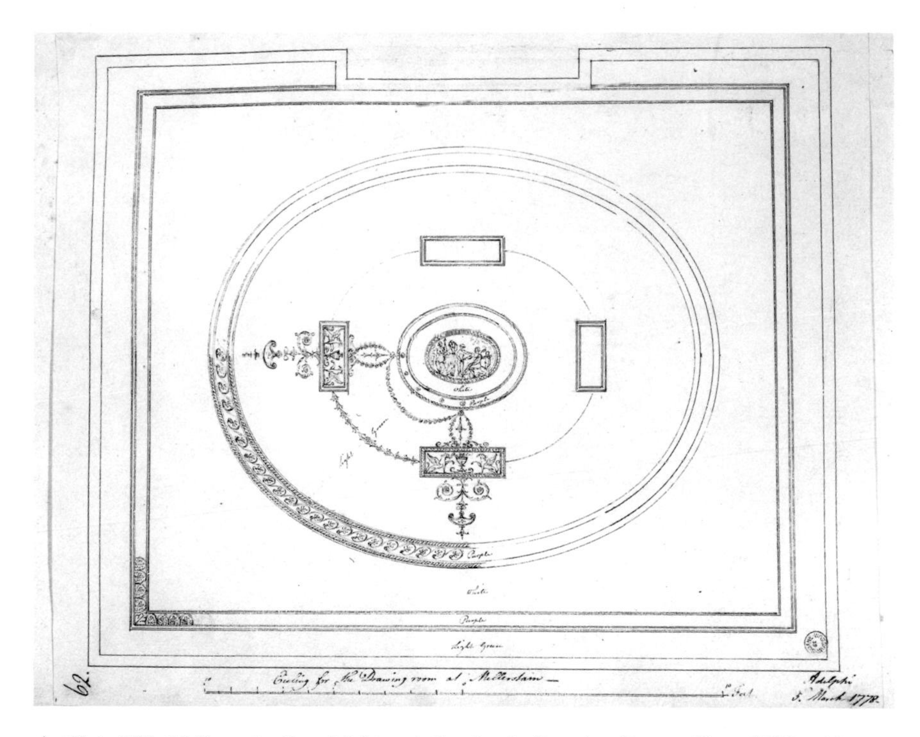

▲ ***Plate 122*** *Mellerstain, Berwickshire, design for the Drawing Room ceiling, 1778, with colour notes. (The Trustees of Sir John Soane's Museum)*

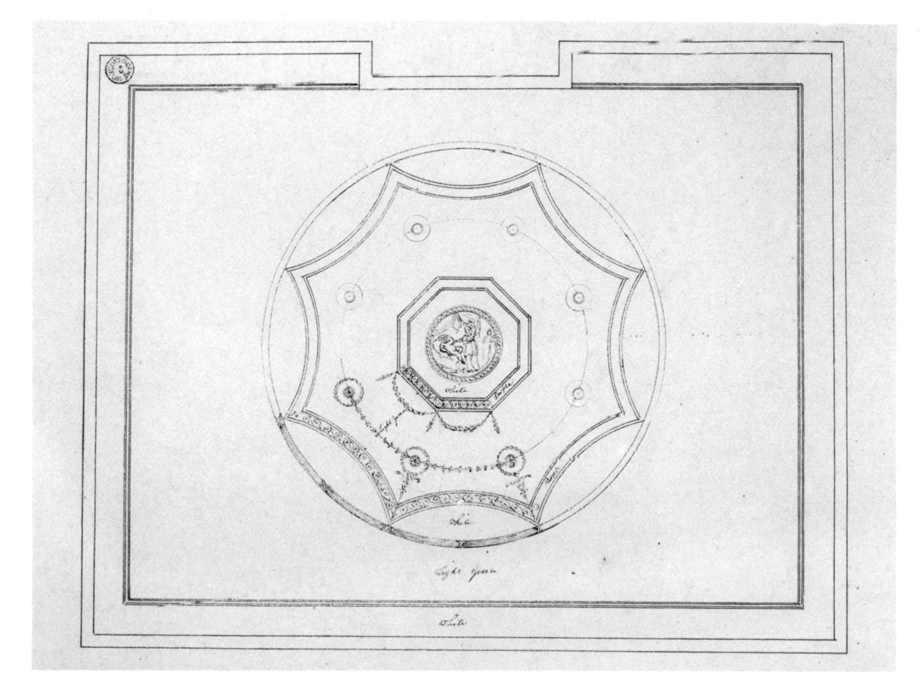

▲ ***Plate 123*** *Mellerstain, Berwickshire, design for the ceiling of the principal Bedchamber, 1778, with colour notes. (The Trustees of Sir John Soane's Museum)*

▲ **Plate 124** *Mellerstain, Berwickshire, Great Gallery on the second floor, general view. (Newbery Smith Photography)*

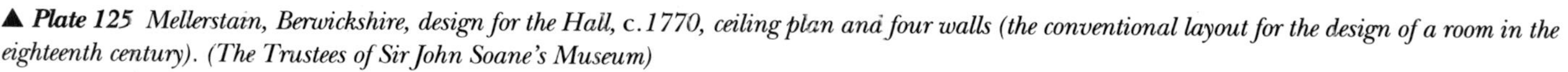

▲ **Plate 125** *Mellerstain, Berwickshire, design for the Hall,* c.1770, *ceiling plan and four walls (the conventional layout for the design of a room in the eighteenth century). (The Trustees of Sir John Soane's Museum)*

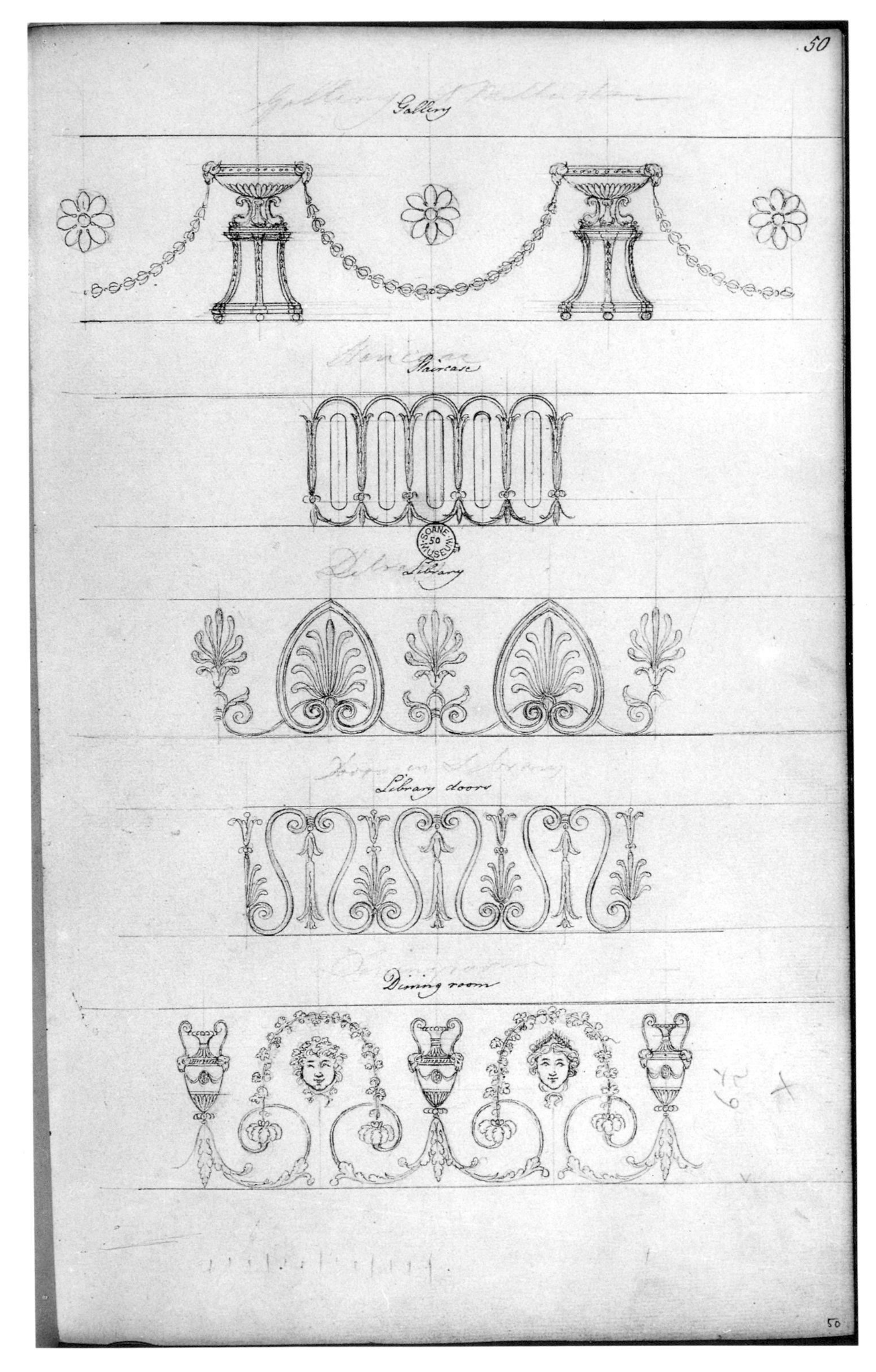

▲ ***Plate 126*** *Mellerstain, Berwickshire, designs for borders,* c.*1778. From top: Gallery, Staircase, Library, Library Doors, Dining Room. (The Trustees of Sir John Soane's Museum)*

▲ **Plate 127** *Mellerstain, Berwickshire, designs for borders,* c.*1778. From top: Drawing Room, Dressing Room, Bed Chamber, Little Dressing Room, Duke of Ancaster (presumably for Grimsthorpe Castle, Lincs). (The Trustees of Sir John Soane's Museum)*

▲ **Plate 128** *Mellerstain, Berwickshire, design for a chimney piece for the Gallery, 1775. (The Trustees of Sir John Soane's Museum)*

▲ **Plate 129** *Mellerstain, Berwickshire, design for a chimney piece for the Dining Room, 1778. (The Trustees of Sir John Soane's Museum)*

The North Front of Mallererstane House Toward the Court. Extends 110 Feet.

▲ **Plate 130** *Mellerstain, Berwickshire, design for the north front, William Adam,* c.1725. *(Royal Commission on the Historical Monuments of Scotland)*

▲ ***Plate 131*** *Poussin,* A Dance to the Music of Time*, c.1637–9, oil on canvas, 83 cm. x 105 cm. (Wallace Collection, London)*

▲ ***Plate 132*** *Claude Lorrain,* Cephalus and Procris reunited by Diana*, 1645, oil on canvas, 102 cm. x 132 cm. (National Gallery, London)*

◀ ***Plate 133*** *David Teniers the Younger,* The Alchemist, *1640s, oil on canvas, 57 cm. x 66.3 cm. (San Diego Museum of Art)*

▼ ***Plate 134*** *David Teniers the Younger,* Fat Kitchen, *1644, oil on canvas, 57 cm. x 77.8 cm. (Mauritshuis, The Hague)*

▲ ***Plate 135*** The Farnese Hercules. *(Mansell Collection, London)*

▲ ***Plate 136*** Antinous. *(Mansell Collection, London)*

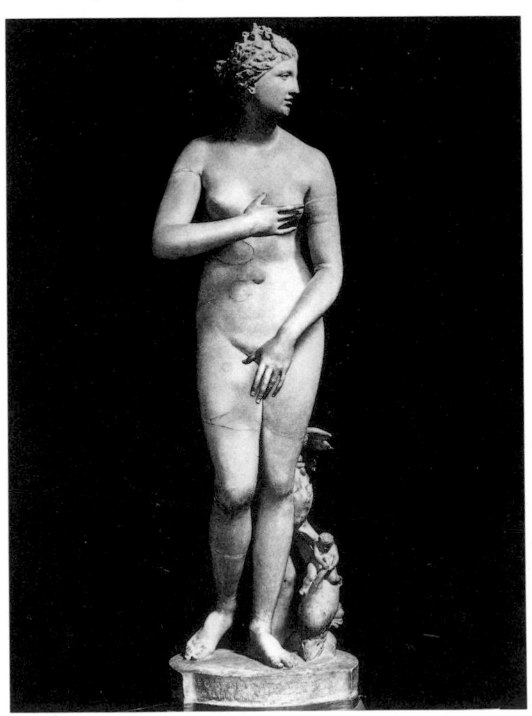

▲ ***Plate 137*** The Medici Venus. *(Mansell Collection, London)*

▲ ***Plate 138*** The Gladiator. *(Mansell Collection, London)*

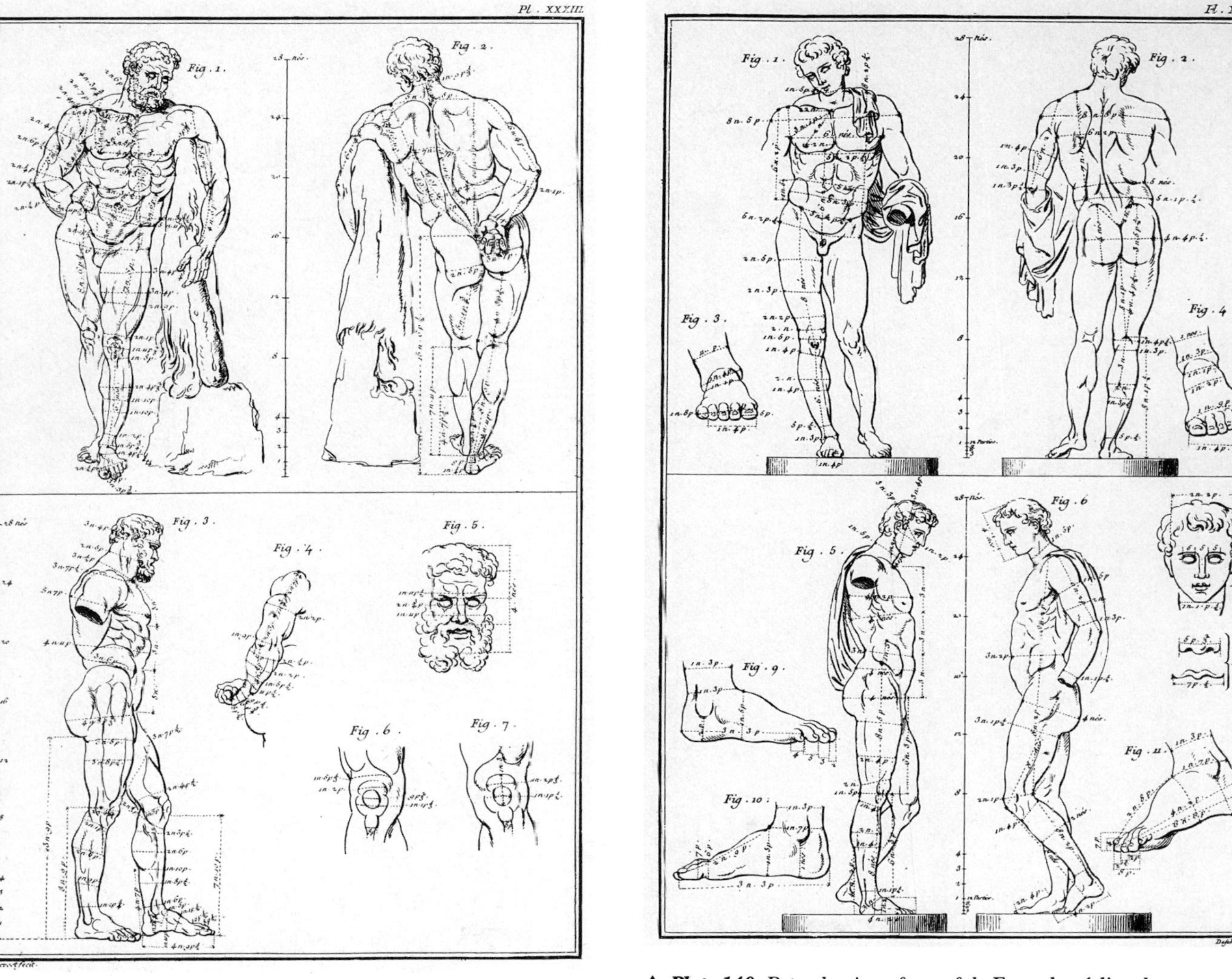

▲ ***Plate 139*** *Reproduction of one of the* Encyclopédie *plates illustrating the article* Drawing (Dessein), *showing the proportions of the Farnese Hercules statue. (Taken from the facsimile edition of the* Encyclopédie, *published by Henri Veyrier, Paris, 1965.)*

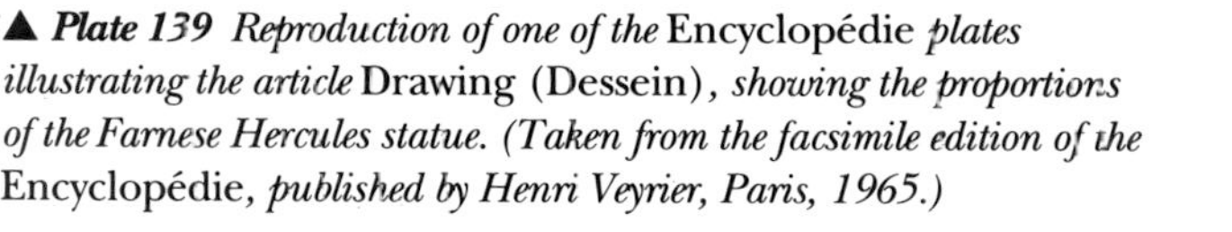

▲ ***Plate 140*** *Reproduction of one of the* Encyclopédie *plates illustrating the article* Drawing (Dessein), *showing the proportions of the Antinous statue. (Taken from the facsimile edition of the* Encyclopédie, *published by Henri Veyrier, Paris, 1965.)*

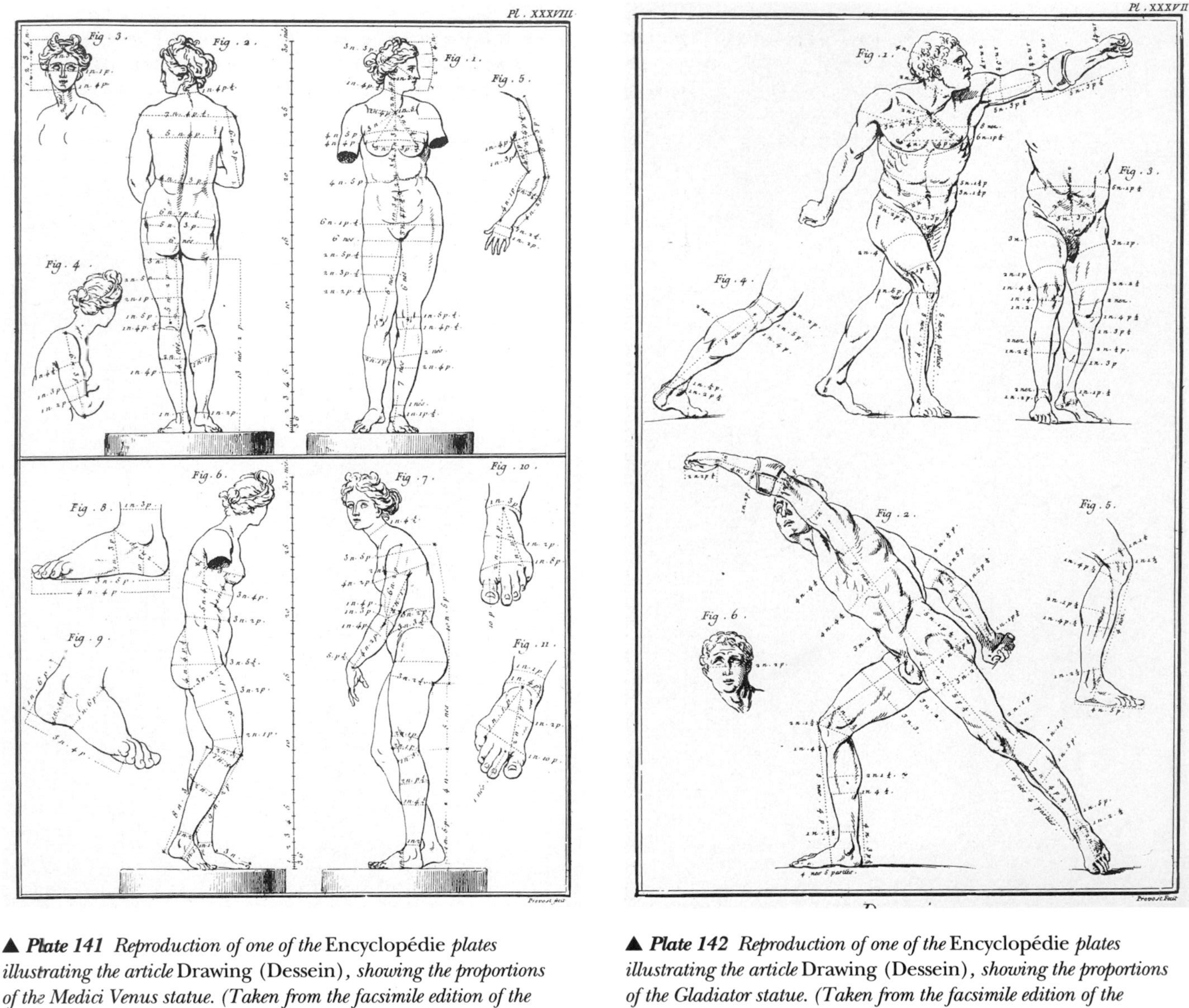

▲ ***Plate 141*** *Reproduction of one of the* Encyclopédie *plates illustrating the article* Drawing (Dessein), *showing the proportions of the Medici Venus statue. (Taken from the facsimile edition of the* Encyclopédie, *published by Henri Veyrier, Paris, 1965.)*

▲ ***Plate 142*** *Reproduction of one of the* Encyclopédie *plates illustrating the article* Drawing (Dessein), *showing the proportions of the Gladiator statue. (Taken from the facsimile edition of the* Encyclopédie, *published by Henri Veyrier, Paris, 1965.)*

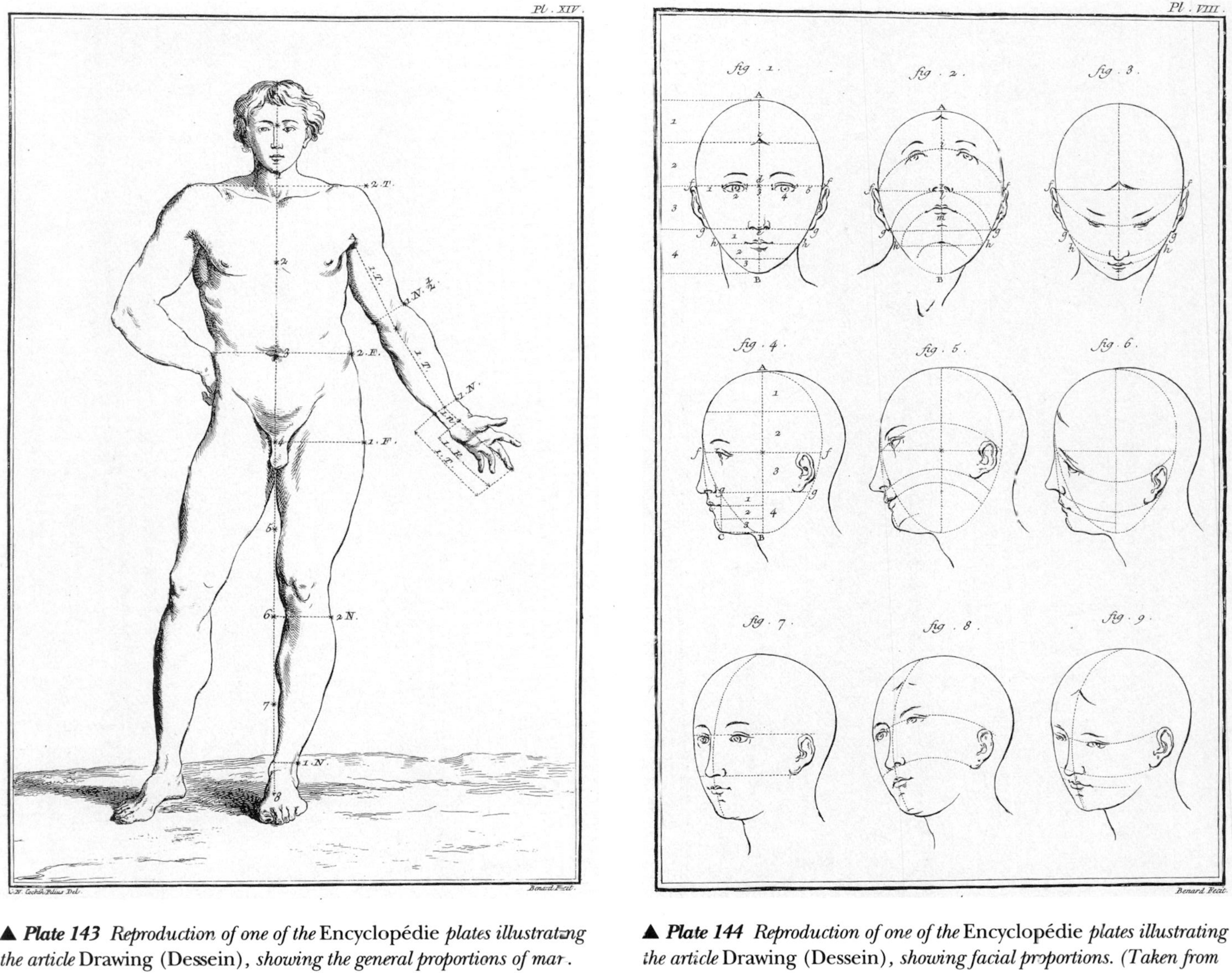

▲ **Plate 143** *Reproduction of one of the* Encyclopédie *plates illustrating the article* Drawing (Dessein), *showing the general proportions of man. (Taken from the facsimile edition of the* Encyclopédie, *published by Henri Veyrier, Paris, 1965.)*

▲ **Plate 144** *Reproduction of one of the* Encyclopédie *plates illustrating the article* Drawing (Dessein), *showing facial proportions. (Taken from the facsimile edition of the* Encyclopédie, *published by Henri Veyrier, Paris, 1965.)*

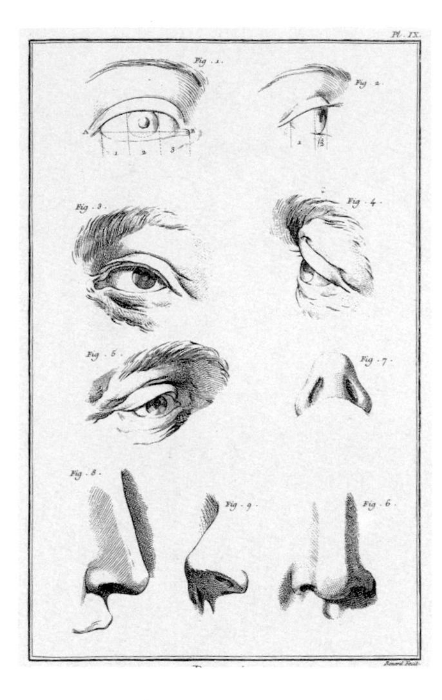

◀ ***Plate 145*** *Reproduction of one of the* Encyclopédie *plates illustrating the article* Drawing (Dessein), *demonstrating the drawing of eyes and noses. (Taken from the facsimile edition of the* Encyclopédie, *published by Henri Veyrier, Paris, 1965.)*

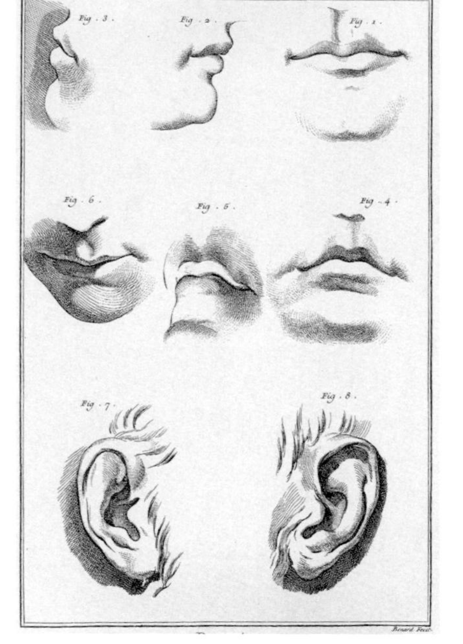

▶ ***Plate 146*** *Reproduction of one of the* Encyclopédie *plates illustrating the article* Drawing (Dessein), *demonstrating the drawing of mouths and ears. (Taken from the facsimile edition of the* Encyclopédie, *published by Henri Veyrier, Paris, 1965.)*

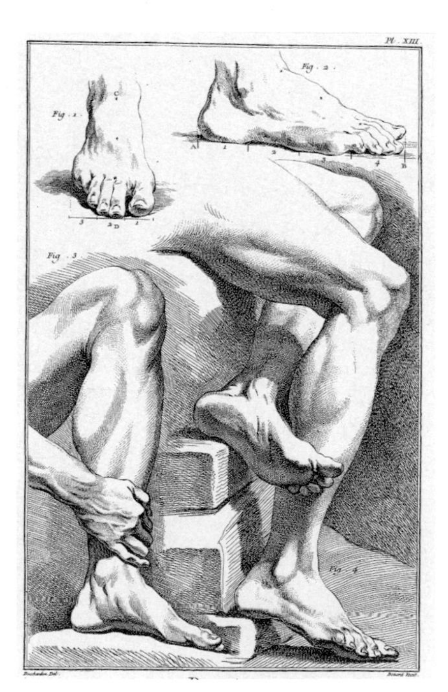

◀ ***Plate 147*** *Reproduction of one of the* Encyclopédie *plates illustrating the article* Drawing (Dessein), *demonstrating the drawing of legs and feet. (Taken from the facsimile edition of the* Encyclopédie, *published by Henri Veyrier, Paris, 1965.)*

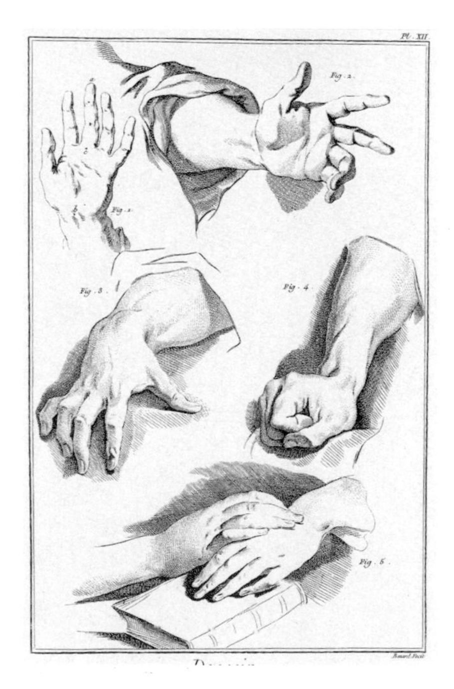

▶ ***Plate 148*** *Reproduction of one of the* Encyclopédie *plates illustrating the article* Drawing (Dessein), *demonstrating the drawing of hands. (Taken from the facsimile edition of the* Encyclopédie, *published by Henri Veyrier, Paris, 1965.)*

◀ **_Plate 149_** _Reproduction of one of the_ Encyclopédie _plates illustrating the article_ Drawing (Dessein), _showing study from the model. (Taken from the facsimile edition of the_ Encyclopédie, _published by Henri Veyrier, Paris, 1965.)_

▶ **_Plate 150_** _Reproduction of one of the_ Encyclopédie _plates illustrating the article_ Drawing (Dessein), _showing study from the model. (Taken from the facsimile edition of the_ Encyclopédie, _published by Henri Veyrier, Paris, 1965.)_

◀ **_Plate 151_** _Reproduction of one of the_ Encyclopédie _plates illustrating the article_ Drawing (Dessein), _showing study from the model. (Taken from the facsimile edition of the_ Encyclopédie, _published by Henri Veyrier, Paris, 1965.)_

▶ **_Plate 152_** _Reproduction of one of the_ Encyclopédie _plates illustrating the article_ Drawing (Dessein), _showing study from the model. (Taken from the facsimile edition of the_ Encyclopédie, _published by Henri Veyrier, Paris, 1965.)_

◀ ***Plate 153*** *Reproduction of one of the* Encyclopédie *plates illustrating the article* Drawing (Dessein), *showing study from the model. (Taken from the facsimile edition of the* Encyclopédie, *published by Henri Veyrier, Paris, 1965.)*

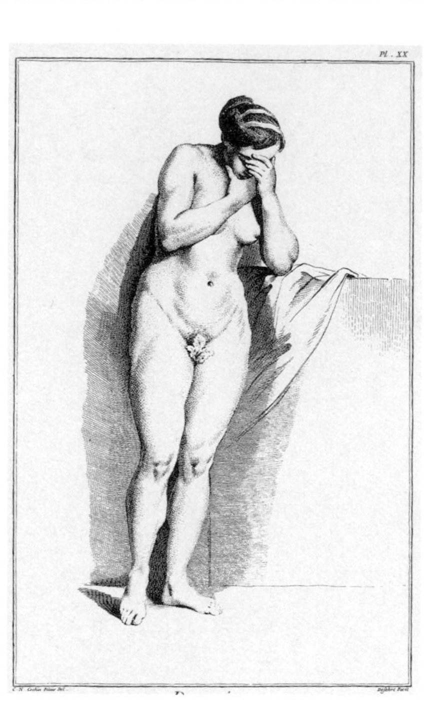

▶ ***Plate 154*** *Reproduction of one of the* Encyclopédie *plates illustrating the article* Drawing (Dessein), *showing study from the model. (Taken from the facsimile edition of the* Encyclopédie, *published by Henri Veyrier, Paris, 1965.)*

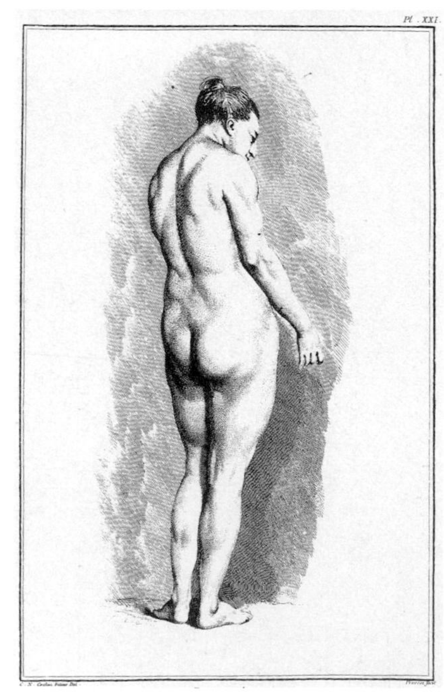

◀ ***Plate 155*** *Reproduction of one of the* Encyclopédie *plates illustrating the article* Drawing (Dessein), *showing study from the model. (Taken from the facsimile edition of the* Encyclopédie, *published by Henri Veyrier, Paris, 1965.)*

▶ ***Plate 156*** *Reproduction of one of the* Encyclopédie *plates illustrating the article* Drawing (Dessein), *showing study from the model. (Taken from the facsimile edition of the* Encyclopédie, *published by Henri Veyrier, Paris, 1965.)*

▲ ***Plate 157*** *Etching from Carle Van Loo,* Six studies from the model, c.*1743.*
(Photo: Bibliothèque Nationale, Paris)

▲ ***Plate 158*** *Etching from Carle Van Loo,* Six studies from the model, c.*1743. (Photo: Bibliothèque Nationale, Paris)*

▲ ***Plate 159*** *Charles-Nicolas Cochin,* The drawing academy, *1763. (Taken from the facsimile edition of the* Encyclopédie, *published by Henri Veyrier, Paris, 1965.)*

▲ ***Plate 160*** *Charles-Nicolas Cochin,* The life class, *c.1760, chalk on paper. (Photographie Bulloz, Paris).*

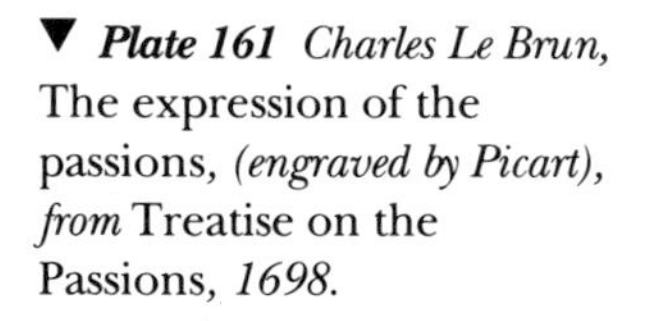

▼ ***Plate 161*** *Charles Le Brun,* The expression of the passions, *(engraved by Picart), from* Treatise on the Passions, *1698.*

▲ ***Plate 162*** *Joseph Vernet,* Morning, *1765, oil on canvas, 108 cm. x 147 cm.*

▲ ***Plate 163*** *Joseph Vernet,* Mid-day. A Storm, *1765, oil on canvas, 115 cm. x 150 cm. (Louvre, Paris. Cliché des Musées Nationaux)*

▲ ***Plate 164*** *Joseph Vernet,* Evening, *oil on canvas, 108 cm. x 148 cm. (Louvre, Paris. Cliché des Musées Nationaux)*

▲ ***Plate 165*** *Joseph Vernet,* Moonlight, *oil on canvas, 108 cm. x 147 cm. (Louvre, Paris. Cliché des Musées Nationaux)*

▲ ***Plate 166*** *Joseph Vernet,* View of Nogent-sur-Seine, *1764, oil on canvas, 76 cm. x 135 cm. (Staatliche Museen, Preussischer Kulturbeisitz, Gemäldegalerie, Berlin)*

▲ ***Plate 167*** *Joseph Vernet,* Great storm, *engraving. (Bibliothèque Nationale)*

▲ **Plate 168** *Joseph Vernet,* Shipwreck by moonlight, *engraving. (Bibliothèque Nationale)*

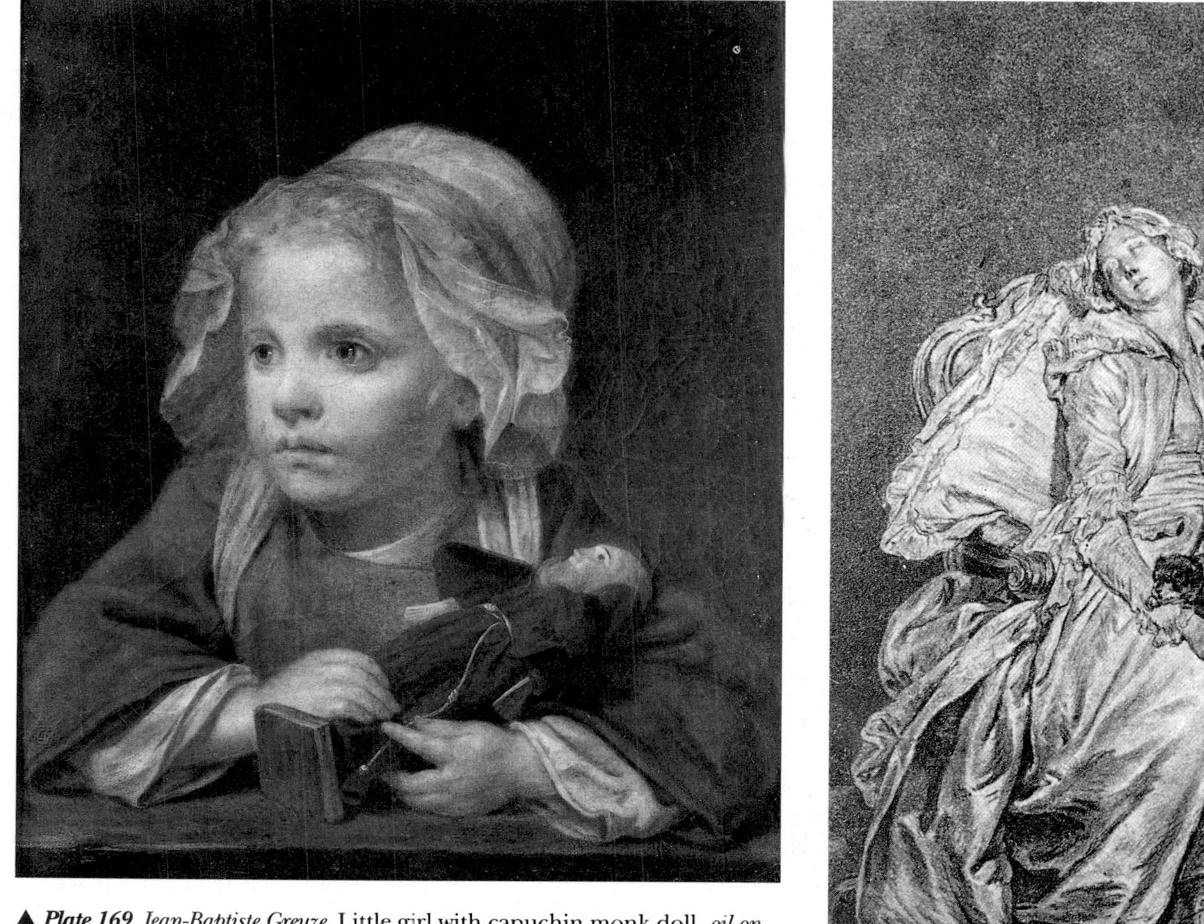

▲ **Plate 169** *Jean-Baptiste Greuze*, Little girl with capuchin monk doll, *oil on canvas, 45.5 cm. x 37.5 cm. (Musée Ingrès, Montauban, Photo: Photographie Giraudon). This is a copy of the painting discussed by Diderot in the Salon of 1765.*

▲ **Plate 170** *Jean-Baptiste Greuze*, Portrait of Madame Greuze, *drawing. (Collection P. Hatvany)*

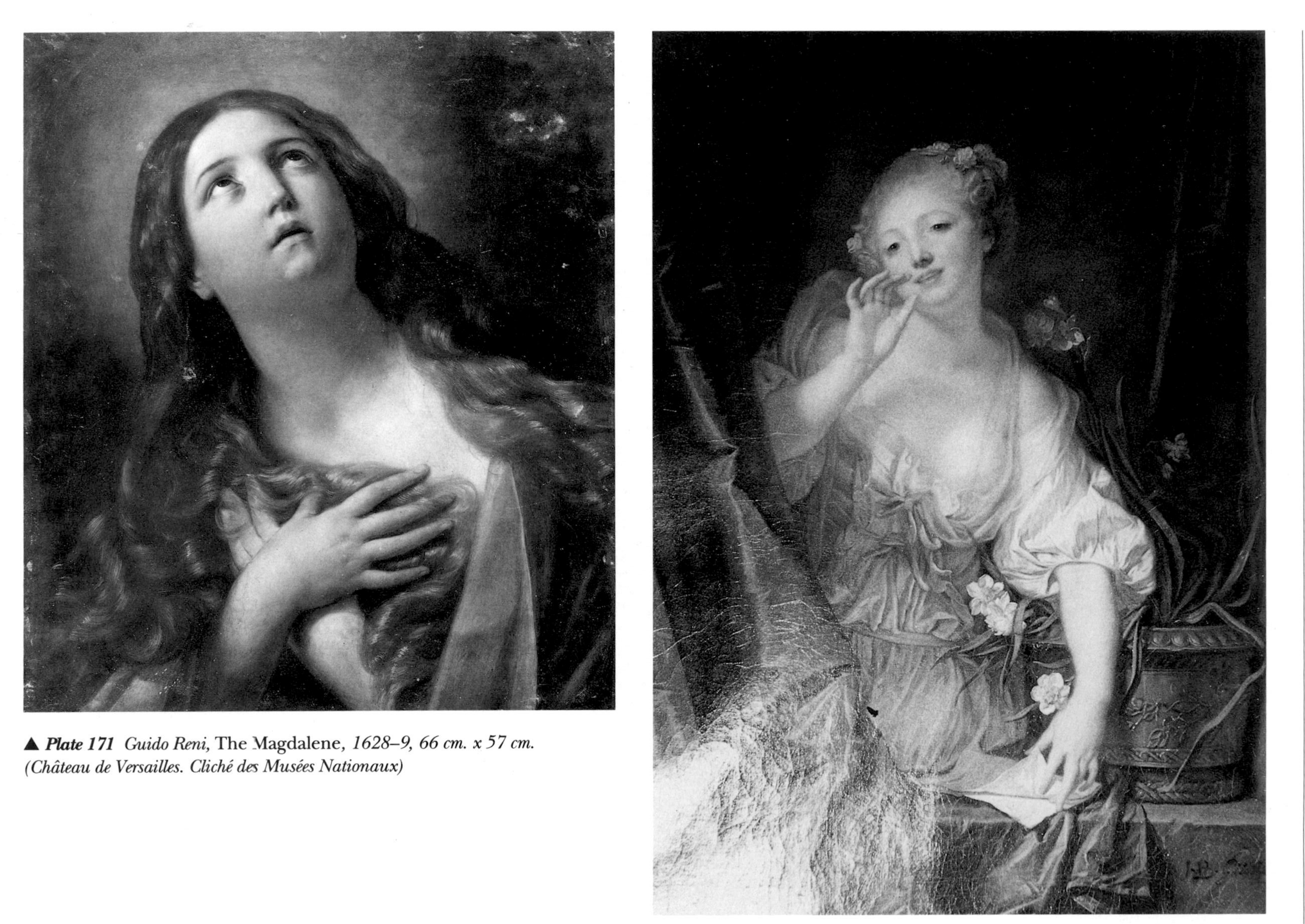

▲ **Plate 171** *Guido Reni,* The Magdalene, *1628–9, 66 cm. x 57 cm. (Château de Versailles. Cliché des Musées Nationaux)*

▲ **Plate 172** *Jean-Baptiste Greuze,* The Kiss, *oil on canvas. (Private Collection)*

◀ ***Plate 173*** *Jean-Baptiste Greuze,* The well-beloved mother, *1765, oil on canvas, 99 cm. x 131 cm. (Laborde Collection, Paris)*

◀ ***Plate 174*** *Jean-Baptiste Le Prince,* Russian pastoral, *oil on canvas, 93.1 cm. x74.1cm. (Photo: Photographie Giraudon)*

▲ ***Plate 175*** *Nicolas Bernard L'Epicié,* The baptism of Jesus Christ, *1763, 250 cm. x 217 cm. (Musée de Caen)*

▶ ***Plate 176*** *Jacques-François Amand,* Joseph sold by his brothers, *1765, oil on canvas, 144 cm. x 177 cm. (Besançon (France), Musée des Beaux-Arts et d'Archéologie)*

▲ ***Plate 177*** *Francois Boucher,* Jupiter transformed into Diana, *oil on canvas. (National Gallery of Art, Washington)*

▲ ***Plate 178*** *François Boucher,* Angélique et Médor, *1763, oil on canvas, 65 cm. x 55 cm. (Ananoff)*

▲ ***Plate 179*** *Francois Boucher,* The dispatch of the messenger, *1765, oil on canvas, 32.1 cm. x 26.7 cm. (Metropolitan Museum of Art, New York)*

▲ ***Plate 180*** *Francois Boucher,* The arrival of the post, *engraving. (Ananoff)*

▲ ***Plate 181*** *Francois Boucher,* Reading the letter, *engraving, 405 cm. x 351 cm. (Ananoff)*

▲ ***Plate 182*** *Francois Boucher,* Are they thinking about this sheep?, *engraving, 405 cm. x 351 cm. (Ananoff)*

▲ ***Plate 183*** *Baudouin,* The Empty Quiver, *engraving.*
(Photo: Photographie Bulloz.)

▲ ***Plate 184*** *Pierre-Antoine Baudouin,* The Cherry Picker, *27 cm. x 22cm.*
(Private Collection, courtesy of Rosenberg & Stiebel, Inc.)

◄ ***Plate 185*** *Baudouin,* Girl scolded by her mother, *engraving. (Bibliothèque Nationale, Paris. Photo: Photographie Giraudon)*

▲ ***Plate 186*** *David,* The oath of the Horatii, *1785, 330 cm. x 425 cm. (Louvre, Paris. Photo: Photographie Giraudon)*

▲ ***Plate 187*** *Jean-Baptiste-Siméon Chardin,* The Attributes of the Arts, *1765, oil on canvas, 91 cm. x 145 cm. (Louvre, Paris. Cliché des Musées Nationaux)*

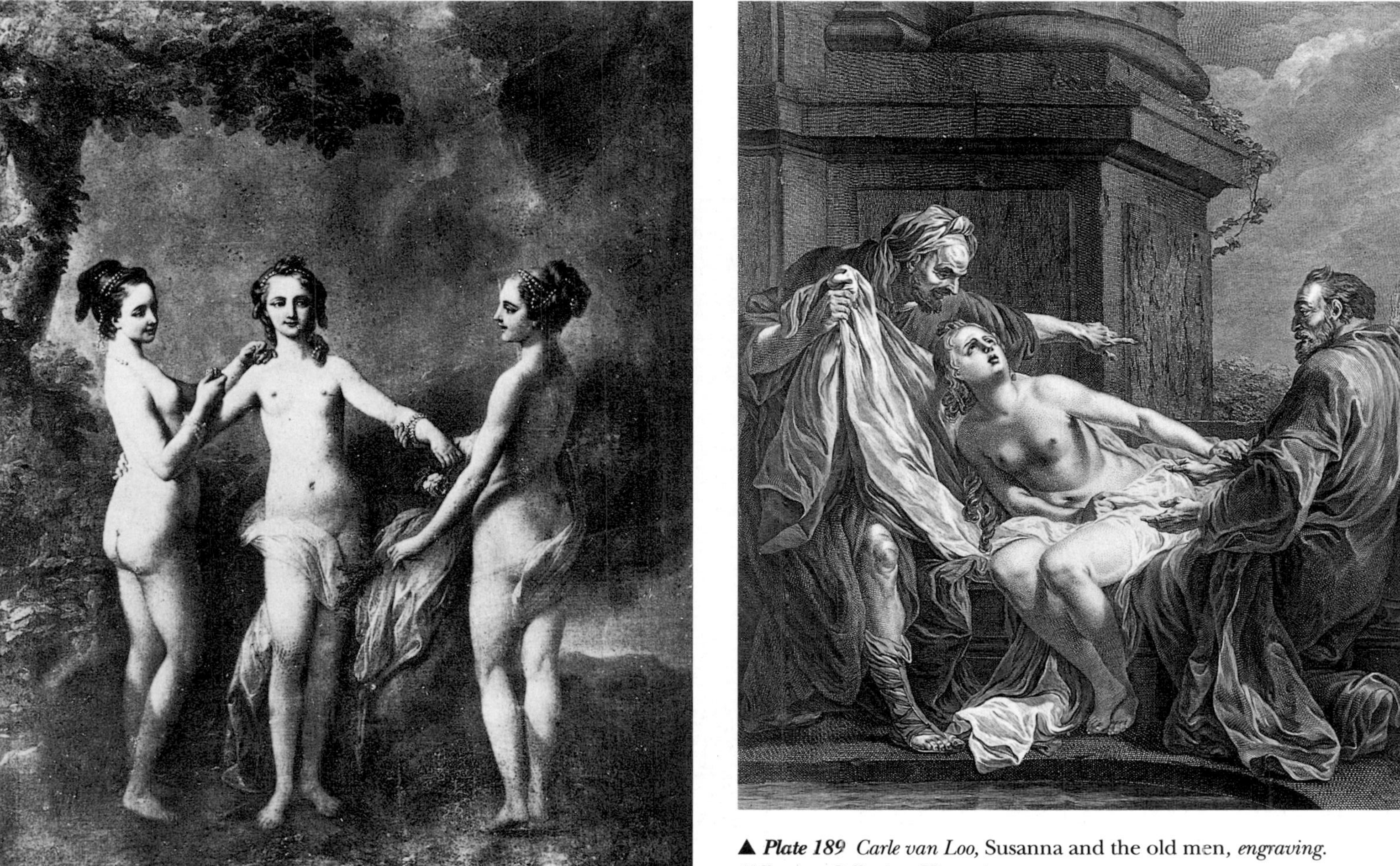

▲ ***Plate 188*** *Carle van Loo,* The Graces, *1765, oil on canvas, 225 cm. x 185 cm. (Château de Chenouceaux)*

▲ ***Plate 189*** *Carle van Loo,* Susanna and the old men, *engraving. (Albertina Collection, Vienna)*

▲ ***Plate 190*** *Carle van Loo,* Saint Gregory dictating his homilies, *sketch, oil on canvas, 101 cm. x 65 cm.* (Burlington Mag.)